NEW MUSIC

NEW MUSIC

A TRILOGY

Reynolds Price

Theatre Communications Group

New Music is published by Theatre Communications Group, Inc., 355 Lexington Ave., New York, NY 10017.

TCG gratefully acknowledges public funds from the National Endowment for the Arts and the New York State Council on the Arts in addition to the generous support of the following foundations and corporations: Alcoa Foundation; ARCO Foundation; AT&T Foundation; Beatrice Foundation; Citibank; Common Wealth Fund; Consolidated Edison Company of New York; Eleanor Naylor Dana Charitable Trust; Dayton Hudson Foundation; Exxon Corporation; Ford Foundation; James Irvine Foundation; Jerome Foundation; Andrew W. Mellon Foundation; Metropolitan Life Foundation; National Broadcasting Company; New York Times Company Foundation; Pew Charitable Trusts; Philip Morris Companies; Reed Foundation; Scherman Foundation; Shell Oil Company Foundation; Shubert Foundation; Lila Wallace-Reader's Digest Fund.

Back cover photograph copyright © 1990 by Will McIntyre.

Library of Congress Cataloging-in-Publication Data
Price, Reynolds, 1933-
New music : a trilogy / Reynolds Price.
Contents: August snow — Night music — Better days.
ISBN 1-55936-015-1 (Cloth)   ISBN 1-55936-016-X (pbk.)
I. Title.
PS3566.R54N48   1990   90-48090
812'.54—dc20   CIP

Design and composition by The Sarabande Press

First Edition, November 1990

CONTENTS

AUGUST SNOW

August 1937

ACT ONE

1

Six o'clock in the morning. Clear weak light seeps through the shaded windows of a large one-room apartment—sturdy Victorian oak furniture, a kitchen corner, a wide bedstead, a reclined Morris chair. Taw Avery is asleep in the chair, wrapped in a cotton quilt, her back to the audience.

A door opens silently and Neal Avery enters. Since leaving work the previous evening, he has drunk a great deal of corn liquor; but the only visible hint is a slow gravity in his movements. He walks to the bed and leans on its foot.

Taw has apparently heard nothing.

NEAL

I estimate you will be bent double by New Year's Eve if you spend one more night in that damned chair.

TAW

(Still not turning but clearly audible) Good. I can pick up pennies off the road.

NEAL

Taw, you're out of the orphanage. You married good money— hell, I've rented this grand bed and all these sheets. *(Waves behind him as if Taw can see)*

TAW

(Turns and sits up. She is fully dressed in last night's clothes) You rent it for *us*, Neal. When you're here, I join you. I promised you that in the only wedding I hope to have. When you vanish, I'd rather sleep cold on the ground.

NEAL

(Thinks, then shudders and hugs himself) I think I slept several hours on the ground since I saw you last.

TAW

(Rising and moving toward the washstand) That's none of my fault. *(Pours water from the pitcher into the bowl and begins to wash her face)*

NEAL

Never claimed it was. But I'm begging your pardon.

Taw continues to wash and dry, then to comb her hair. She walks to the kitchen corner—a stove, an old icebox, an enamel dishpan, a water bucket. She takes one egg from a bowl on the shelf, then turns to Neal.

TAW

Could you eat a fresh egg if I soft-boil it for you?

NEAL

You never said you pardon me.

TAW

I don't—yet—Neal.

NEAL

Then I couldn't swallow, no. *(Moves to sit on the side of the bed)* No ma'm, not today.

TAW

You're going to need your full strength today.

NEAL

No ma'm, not for *sleep*. *(Lies back on the bed)*

TAW

(Returns the egg to its bowl) You can't sleep here. *(When Neal fails to respond, she advances to the table in the midst of the room)* Don't sleep here, Neal—not today. Please listen.

NEAL

Make it peaceful, Taw.

TAW

I can't. Not now.

Neal rises to his elbows and faces her, unsmiling.

TAW

This room is all yours, if you plan to claim it. But I'm asking you to leave here now and let us both think through our mess in some kind of calm. *(Sits at the table)* Neal, I've *thought*. I know what I can do. I can wait here till time for supper this evening.

You go off and think about our year together and the time to come. Then if you know I'm the person you need to spend long years with, come back by dark; and I'll start cooking ham and boiling rice.

NEAL

Let me get this plain—you want me to think about what *you* want, the thing you want me to turn into?

TAW

I want you to be a good person, that's all.

NEAL

But *your* good person—a house-broke dog. *(Rises, goes to the table and sits opposite Taw)*

TAW

(Waits, then nods) House-broke, if that means coming home at sundown to eat and rest—not filthy and sick, not twelve hours late and a good supper ruined, your wife not knowing if you're sick or dead.

You *need* to be drunk two or three nights a week? You need to break every promise you made to stand by me?

NEAL

"Forsaking all others"? Did I say that?

TAW

To God and every old lady in town, in the Presbyterian church one evening a whole year ago. I *promised* you, Neal. And you promised me.

NEAL

(Laughs) I was drunk then too.

TAW

No excuse.

NEAL

(Laughs again) I couldn't hear the vows — Porter cried so loud.

TAW

(Almost smiles) You've nearly got a point. Porter should've been shot.

NEAL

No harm in a man's best friend shedding tears when the man takes a wife.

TAW

(Nods her head slowly as if to agree) You sure you took me?

NEAL

It felt like you. You claimed you liked it.

TAW

I liked *you* in it, when you were there and sober. I wouldn't give two cents to do it with any other man alive.

NEAL

How much you give me to do it right now? I'm here and ready.

TAW

(Studies him, incredulous) I paid you, every dollar you cost. I've offered you my whole life to spend.

NEAL

(Smiles) At pretty good interest. On your little terms.

TAW

(Stands in bafflement, walks to the bed, smooths the wrinkles in the cover, then stands at the foot) If loyal attention is little, all right—and keeping your mind clear enough to guide you home in the dark—then sure, I'm one of the littlest dwarfs.

Neal stands and moves as if to approach her.

TAW

No. Leave like I asked you. If you turn up for supper, on your own two feet and nobody with you, I'll know you want us to keep on together. Otherwise, I'll pack and be gone by morning.

NEAL

Where to?

TAW

There's more than one place for clean young people that are sober round-the-clock and always know their name and address and can be leaned on.

NEAL

You'd die.

TAW

I'd die being true to what I know.

Neal moves to sit again at the table.

TAW

Please get out. It'll be all yours, one way or another, by dark tonight.

NEAL

(Takes three steps away, turns) Should I say goodbye?

TAW

No—well, at least for now. *(Waits)* I grew up alone. I can't think like you, in a room full of people all joking and mean. Just give me today to think my way clear. You please do the same. Tonight we can cancel goodbye if we're ready.

NEAL

Stop drinking, stop seeing my oldest friend, and be just yours?
That's all I've got to decide by supper?

TAW

More or less. It's time.

NEAL

Swear to God, I thought we were doing all right—*I'm* happy.

TAW

I'm not. And you've known it for long months. If not, you're
blinder than I ever dreamed. *(Waves slowly around her, the
whole still room)* Neal, I never meant this. I never planned *this*.

NEAL

Taw, you can't plan life.

TAW

You can. I've done it. And it was not *this*.

NEAL

*(Waits, then reaches slowly out in the empty air as if to touch
her)* All right. Goodbye.

TAW

We've got till supper—

NEAL

(Nods) Goodbye.

Taw gives a small wave.

Neal quietly leaves, not looking back.

2

Immediately after Neal's departure, Taw moves to the table and sits in the chair facing the audience. Her speech is an unashamed soliloquy.

TAW

Since I was an orphan so early in life, I taught myself to avoid most dreams — dreams at night, good or bad. They seemed one strain I could spare myself; and I honestly think, in all these years, I've never had two dozen dreams — not to speak of. Neal dreams like a dog by the stove when he's here, the rare nights I get to guard his sleep. Last night though when I finally dozed, sad as I was, I lived through a dream as real as day.

I'd finished my teacher's diploma and was ready to save the world around me, all children. What thrilled me was *that* — they were all young and not too hard yet to help. I'd show them the main thing an orphan knows — how to tuck your jaw and brave hails of pain and come out strong as a good drayhorse or a rock-ribbed house on a cliff by water.

But once I entered my class the first day and trimmed my pencil and faced the desks, I saw they'd given me twenty grown men — all with straight sets of teeth. I prayed I was wrong, that I'd got the wrong room. Still I said my name, and the oldest man at the back of the room stood tall at last in a black serge suit and said "Don't wait another minute to start. We've paid our way."

I had a quick chill of fright that I'd fail; but then I thought of the week they died — my mother and father, of Spanish flu — and I knew I did have a big truth to tell, the main one to know.

I opened my mouth and taught those grown men every last fact an orphan needs and learns from the day she's left — courage and trust and a craving for time. They listened too but hard as I looked in all the rows, I never saw Neal.

3

*Immediately after. The kitchen of Roma Avery, Neal's mother—
an out-of-date but tidy room: late Victorian oak furniture (a
table and chairs, a sizable rocker), adequate electrical ap-
pliances and other cooking gear of the time. Porter Farwell
stands at the range, scrambling eggs. He is dressed for work, his
jacket on a chair; but he cooks with unhurried competence, no
wasted moves.*

   Roma enters in nightgown and bathrobe.

   Porter does not hear her.

ROMA

You're taking kitchen privileges, I see.

PORTER

(Surprised) Oh yes ma'm. I didn't see any point in calling you.

ROMA

And no point either in not telling me you planned not to spend
last night in your room? I barely shut an eye.

PORTER

By the time I knew where I'd be, it was too late to call.

ROMA

Porter, cast your mind back. I rented you Neal's room the day
he left so I wouldn't lie here helpless at night to any passing
felon.

PORTER

Let me fix you some of my feather-light eggs.

ROMA

Just coffee please.

Roma sits at the head of the table.

*Porter serves Roma coffee, then brings his own plate of eggs and
sits at her right.*

PORTER

Mrs. Avery, I'd bet a day's pay you were truly the only eye open in town after midnight.

ROMA

Half the world's rapes are over by midnight.

PORTER

I won't doubt your word. I know how hard you've researched the subject. *(Begins to eat)*

ROMA

Porter, recall I'm much your elder and a recent widow. Show some respect. *(Tastes the coffee, frowns hard but continues drinking)* Since I was the only soul awake, where was your sleepy head? And my son's, may I ask?

PORTER

You asked us to check on your dogs, remember?

ROMA

The hounds of the Dear Departed, not mine.

PORTER

He'd be pleased to see how well they've done.

ROMA

He'd be mad as hell. Britt Avery hoped we'd all roll round— dogs included—prostrate with grief, ever after he died.

PORTER

Well, the dogs are grand—not one tearful eye. Of course, old Turner doesn't hunt them enough. They're plump as ladies and doze all day. They've hatched a few puppies—you own sixteen fine fox-dogs today.

ROMA

You and Neal better hunt them to the bone this fall; or I plan to give one each, in person, to the first sixteen honest children I meet in the road.

PORTER

How will you know the honest ones?

ROMA

(Studies her face in the back of a spoon) I'll ask them to describe my looks in five words. Anybody not saying "Ugly as a scalded rabbit" *(Counts the words on her fingers)* gets no hound dog.

PORTER

Mrs. Avery, you forget we married Neal off. Now we've got to help him put away childish things.

ROMA

(Takes up a large salt shaker, slowly unscrews the top) And sit down in one rented room, no private bath, while Miss Taw Sefton preaches her sermons on true love and virtue?

PORTER

She's Mrs. Neal Avery now, for some reason.

ROMA

Ask her; ask Taw—she'll tell you all day and into the night. *Neal* could no more tell you than this salt could. *(Ceremoniously empties the shaker into her palm—a damp teaspoon of salt—then shuts her fingers on it)*

PORTER

He *wants* her, right now.

ROMA

(Rises, moves toward the sink) Then stand back; it's love.

PORTER

Ma'm?

ROMA

You just defined *love*—hot need, right *now.*

PORTER

Then anybody's love can end any day.

ROMA

(Brushes salt from her hand) I think you'll find that's a fact about love they don't advertise.

PORTER

I doubt I believe you.

ROMA

Then don't grow up.

Neal stands in the door.

Porter senses him and turns; they nod, unsmiling.

PORTER

(To Roma) Your wandering boy's hungry.

ROMA

(Not facing Neal) He's not mine now.

NEAL

You're dead-wrong—I'm not a bit hungry. But Mother, I'm yours.

ROMA

Try the Salvation Army.

PORTER

Sit here; you're pale. I saved you some eggs.

Porter stands and goes to the oven for eggs.

Neal walks to his mother, kisses her neck. Then he sits in her place at the head of the table.

Porter serves him while Roma stands to watch.

ROMA

(As Neal takes the first mouthful) That's *my* chair.

NEAL

It was Father's, then mine.

ROMA

(Moving toward him) And both of you quit it. *(Stands at Neal's side)*

Neal rises and moves his plate beyond Porter, then quietly sits.

Roma sits again and smiles.

ROMA

Thank you, son.

NEAL

I may reclaim it.

ROMA

(*Laughs*) It would have to be earned.

All turn for a moment to their plates and cups.

PORTER

You fix things at home?

NEAL

Taw's all right.

They eat and drink again.

ROMA

I haven't heard the rest of where you laid those two clever heads
last night. I mean, after you'd seen my big fat dogs—not at
Taw's, I take it.

Porter looks first to Neal, then gestures toward him.

NEAL

Mother, you'll live years longer not knowing.

ROMA

My people live *far* into their nineties. I've been wife to a half-
mute skinflint, mother to a souse; and now I'm heir to a men's
clothing store that's showing a profit for the first year in ten. So
sure, hit me hard; I doubt I'll break.

NEAL

(*To Porter*) How much have you told her?

PORTER

Just the dogs.

NEAL

Old Turner, you can guess, has time on his hands—his wife

and mother-in-law do the farming, and his girl feeds the dogs.
So when we got there, he had just finished making a dugout
canoe—burnt from a cypress log and lovely as somebody's neat
strong leg.

You know I've wanted one all my life; so I offered him five
dollars for it, on the spot. He moaned and bragged for half an
hour, then took eight dollars and my old nailclippers in exchange for something even you would love. *(Pauses to eat)*

ROMA

(Pleased now and beginning to warm) Where is it?

NEAL

Porter, where is it?

PORTER

In thick honeysuckle near where you slept. I hid it at dawn.

NEAL

(To Roma) We took it to the river to test.

ROMA

In night black as Egypt?

NEAL

Porter, was it dark? Yes ma'm, must have been—way past
suppertime. We drove to the sandbar and slid the boat in.
Funny, I remember it all as daylight—good sharp pictures.
Then we just drifted down with the current—what, Porter?—
maybe two miles, past that rock your father used to skin otters
on.

ROMA

My great-grandfather. No otter round here for eighty-odd
years.

NEAL

Porter, weren't you singing every inch of the way?

PORTER

No sir, I was too busy praying not to drown.

NEAL

Never one minute's danger. I could balance on a web, much less the Brown River. And a little past the rock is that notch in the bank with the crippled tree. I landed us there, safe as Captain Cook.

ROMA

Captain Cook was slaughtered in the Sandwich Islands by tattooed natives.

NEAL

I imitate his *better* days. Then we slept—right, Porter?

PORTER

You did, after telling me more than I planned about your honeymoon and other old jokes. I was mainly awake, keeping guard against wolves.

NEAL

Hasn't been a wolf around here since Columbus.

ROMA

Since I was a girl.

PORTER

We're all safe now—send silver donations in lieu of thanks to Porter Farwell.

ROMA

(Smiles) You'll hear from my lawyer. *(To Neal)* And son, I believe you left out the corn.

NEAL

Beg your pardon?

ROMA

Corn liquor. I figure you bought some liquor from Turner and floated that boat and yourselves on corn.

NEAL

Goes without saying.

ROMA

It killed my father.

NEAL

Your father was shot at the wrong back door.

PORTER

Drunk as a goat in love, at the time.

ROMA

Porter, eat your sausage. This is family business.

Porter laughs but obeys.

ROMA

(To Neal) If Miss Taw Sefton drives you to drink, then seize the wheel back. You come from far too long a line of sots.

NEAL

Mother, notice I'm bound to the former Taw Sefton. *(Holds up his ring finger, a single gold band)*

ROMA

Gold will melt in a fire.

PORTER

Whoa! *(Laughs edgily and stands)* Time for work. I mean to go wash my mouth out with soap; you both do the same. *(Sets his dishes in the sink and goes to the door)* Neal, meet you on the porch in three minutes, hear? *(Leaves)*

Neal nods, not looking.

Roma stands and moves more plates to the sink. From there she changes her tone.

ROMA

Son, once you've opened up, call me from the store. We need to talk about winter hats.

NEAL

(Faces round in his chair, nods, stands) This'll be a long day.

ROMA

Eat lunch with me?

NEAL

(Steps toward the door) I'd better not, thank you.

ROMA

Taw coming to meet you?

NEAL

Not today. Got a lot on my mind.

ROMA

Be good to your mind. It started life smart. I know; I made you.

NEAL

(Smiles and shrugs) All right, all right. I won't fight you now.

Neal stands in place a moment, intending his concession to be the last word.

But Roma takes two steps forward and shakes her head.

ROMA

No. Don't.

Neal thinks, then slowly turns, pauses at a shelf and mirror by the door and brushes his hair. Then he leaves.

Roma steps to the table and flicks at crumbs.

4

Just before noon, Taw and Neal's rented room. Taw is freshly dressed, her hair combed neatly, and is taking clothes from a tall wardrobe, rehanging some but choosing others to fold and lay in squared-off piles on the bed. It's a melancholy chore and the imminent chance of real heartbreak marks all her acts, even in the face of her visitor's encouragement.

A knock at the door.

Taw hesitates but unlocks and opens on Genevieve Slappy, their resident landlady, in uncombed hair and housecoat.

TAW

You're up early, Genevieve. It's barely noon.

GENEVIEVE

If I slept fifteen minutes all night, I sure don't recall.

TAW

(Stepping aside to wave her in) I do—you did. (Points to the ceiling) Those hairline cracks in the plaster there? You snore in earnest. (Locks the door)

GENEVIEVE

(Moves toward the icebox) No such thing. I prayed the whole time. You got any chocolate pudding left? (Pats the top of the icebox, not touching the door)

TAW

I ate the last spoonful at four A.M. (Returns to the bed and again sorts clothes)

GENEVIEVE

You don't plan to ask what kept me awake?

TAW

Gen, the whole population south of Boston knows who worries you.

GENEVIEVE

(Laughs) No such thing—I hide my wounds. Who woke you at four?

TAW

Nobody. Nobody.

GENEVIEVE

Neal never showed up.

TAW

You asking or telling? (Smiles) Either case, you're wrong. He showed his drunk face just after dawn.

GENEVIEVE

That's a good deal more than Wayne Watkins showed.

TAW

Wayne is not your husband.

GENEVIEVE

He wants to be.

TAW

Then who please is stopping him?

GENEVIEVE

Don't be mean, Taw. It spoils your skin.

TAW

Help yourself to the rest of the peach pie and sit.

Genevieve opens the icebox, takes out the pie plate, locates a fork, then sits at the central table to eat.

GENEVIEVE

Where had he been now, and what was his story?

TAW

Under the stars with you-know-who, I guess. I didn't ask. I don't trust myself not to break any minute.

GENEVIEVE

You're as likely to break as the pyramids at Giza. When you hold Neal Avery to the line is when you'll *know*.

TAW

Know what?

GENEVIEVE

How much of a life you'll have, from here on.

TAW

A damned sight better life than I've had *this* year—you and Wayne upstairs shredding the rafters while I sat here praying Porter Farwell would return my spouse to these empty arms with no parts missing, as daylight broke.

GENEVIEVE

I apologize for Wayne and me.

TAW

That's not the point. You don't bother me.

GENEVIEVE

The hell it's not. The whole point is how to live close to human beings and not get killed, not kill one of them. *(Waits and wonders if she has pushed too far)*

I didn't plan to say it; but I've lived some, believe me—with more than just Wayne—and Taw, the *point* is what you've missed all along.

TAW

And you see it plainly?

GENEVIEVE

Yes ma'm, I do—to my own heartbreak.

TAW

(Suddenly turning to sit on the bed, among her own clothes) I bet I can guess—two good short mottoes, suitable for stitching: Living Alone Is Worse Than Being Dead; Bear Any Grade of Hell Your Mate Needs to Hand You.

GENEVIEVE

Positively. You can laugh now. I pray you never know first-hand what I know.

TAW

You're what—one whole year older than me? So don't try sounding all-wise yet. And *alone!* I'd have to swear, if called to court, that Wayne Watkins spends more time here than daylight.

GENEVIEVE

Be ashamed. *(But she smiles)* You're wasting too much time as a spy.

TAW

Then get me another job—Neal won't let me teach.

GENEVIEVE

You could start by asking where you've gone wrong to cause a good boy—that I *know's* kind and true—to plow up the world just to prove he's sad. I'm your friend till the devil reclaims me, but I have to say this—Neal used to be happy. People welcomed his face.

TAW

I could welcome him today. *(Rises from the bed, goes to the dining table and slowly sits)* Understand, I'm *proud* to claim I'm the main cause of all this mess he makes. He's run up finally against one human that asks him to give her the best he's got and won't take less.

GENEVIEVE

You're proud of that?

TAW

A little, yes. And Gen, Neal *wanted* it. He knew me two years before he chose me. He knew I couldn't stand a life like this.

GENEVIEVE

And you knew him, knew he was wild in a harmless way— getting tight, taking jaunts for days on end to see some sight in the mountains or a baseball game on donkey-back. More than one person thought Neal killed his father with undue worry but I never did.

His daddy had Roma Avery on his back—she's known to be healthy as a sack of rat-bait. And everybody knew God above tended Neal—Neal's driven off roads into sheer ravines more times than I've made first-class fudge.

TAW

Not with me he hasn't.

GENEVIEVE

Pity on you; you missed a good time. *(Waits, then tentatively)* I told you about the time we had to get the Lightning Calculator to drive us home, didn't I?

TAW

Us?

GENEVIEVE

(Nods) Wayne and I—we were in on some of Neal's best adventures. See, one day Miss Boyd, our algebra teacher, read out a long piece from the paper saying they had this lame boy in Windy, near the mountains; and the boy could watch a whole freight train pass, add up in his head the serial number on the side of each car, then give you the total at the sight of the caboose. He was ten years old and was already called the Lightning Calculator up that way.

I listened and promptly forgot the story. But Saturday night of the same week, we were all at a dance. Most of the boys had already, so to speak, blurred their vision; and I was thinking I might walk home again—my bosoms had finally blossomed, so I wasn't eager to risk harming *them.*

But Neal stepped up—"I'm leaving in a minute for Windy, N.C. I plan to spend Sunday with the Lightning Calculator. Who's coming along?"

Before I could scuttle and strike out for home, Wayne said "I am, me and Genevieve Slappy"—he still likes to use my awful name, however mad it makes me. Before I could breathe, much less say No, we were on the damned highway. All I could do was pray for life and the prayers worked.

TAW

Was the boy awake?

GENEVIEVE

Awake? He was fully dressed and on the porch at daybreak. Neal walked right up and asked when the next freight train was due. Without one word of "Who are you?" or "Go to hell," the Lightning Calculator said "An hour." His real name was Jarvis, Sylvester Jarvis.

His mother appeared at the screen door then and said "Vester, who's all this so early?" Next thing you knew we were eating fried apples and drinking coffee strong enough to ream a radiator.

TAW

Neal was sober by then?

GENEVIEVE

For an hour or two—that's the *end* of the story.

TAW

I may not last.

GENEVIEVE

Do. It's the happy part.

Taw nods and smiles but rises quietly, goes to the wardrobe and resumes her work.

GENEVIEVE

It turned out Vester was eleven not ten, but the lame part was true. His left leg was bowed like the big-letter *C*, and he rolled when he walked. So just before seven he rolled us all back out to the porch, and here came the freight on a fast downgrade.

I could barely see the numbers on the cars, but Sylvester's lips were working top-clip. Neal had squatted beside him. When the last car passed, the child stood up and said "Fourteen million, two hundred twenty thousand and seventy-six."

Wayne and I were speechless with wonder. But Neal just stayed at Vester's bad knee and said "Son, who in the world can *check* you?" Vester gazed off toward a mountain and swallowed. Even the newspaper hadn't caught on. There was nobody fast enough to check the child's total. He could just have been estimating or lying.

TAW

Did Vester fight back?

GENEVIEVE

Not a word. I think he was somehow relieved to be caught. The Lightning Calculator was dead; now he could go on and be just a child. But he shed a few tears. When Wayne said "Lightning, *I* still believe you," Vester turned round and his cheeks were wet.

So out of the wild blue, Neal said "Ace, I bet you can drive " Vester thought a minute and then said "Yeah, I like that name." Neal of course called him *Ace* the whole way home.

TAW

He didn't come with you?

GENEVIEVE

Sugar, Ace *drove* us every mile of the way. We were all asleep, trusting as babes.

TAW

Did his mother know?

GENEVIEVE

Knew and made three dollars on the deal. Neal gave her that much as we drove off; and he sent Ace home on the evening train with a brand-new hacksaw over his shoulder, which was all he wanted by way of a present.

TAW

I guess he's gone on to rob trains and banks.

GENEVIEVE

(Waits) That wasn't my point, Taw, I'm sad to say.

TAW

(Smiles) Write it out then and mail it to me.

GENEVIEVE

Neal's—a—funny—kind—soul.

TAW

Why did *you* pass him up?

GENEVIEVE

I've loved a lot of people, but I just wanted Wayne. *(Laughs)* And of course I never got a chance at Neal.

TAW

May have been the best luck you'll ever have.

Genevieve waits, then rises slowly and walks to Taw. When

they are face to face, both unsmiling, Genevieve puts out a gentle hand and covers Taw's mouth.

GENEVIEVE

Take that back right now while you can.

Genevieve retracts her hand.

Taw shakes her head No.

The hall door rattles; someone tries to enter. Silence, then a knock, then Neal's voice.

NEAL

Taw—

Genevieve's hand goes up for a second touch at Taw's mouth.

But Taw steps back, shakes her head No harder. Then she moves to the door, turns the key and opens it.

Neal is still in yesterday's clothes; but his face is clean, his hair brushed down.

TAW

You found a hairbrush at least.

NEAL

I stopped by home.

TAW

Where is that?

NEAL

(Points) My mother's.

TAW

Then what's this room?

Neal steps past her and smiles at Genevieve.

Genevieve gives a little-girl curtsey in reply.

NEAL

(Turns back to Taw) This is the room we rented from my friend
Genevieve Slappy to start our life.

GENEVIEVE

And Genevieve's leaving. Enjoy your lunch.

Genevieve steps briskly to the door.

Neal sees the stacks of clothes on the bed and goes to touch them.

Genevieve whispers goodbye to Taw.

Taw shuts the door behind her, not locking it now.

*Neal lifts up a cardigan sweater of Taw's and holds it before
him.*

NEAL

You having a sale?

TAW

No.

NEAL

*(Holds up a single arm of the sweater, clasps the body to him
and dances two steps)* Inventory?

TAW

I told you I might have to pack tonight—so, sure, *inventory.* All
of it's mine.

*Facing Taw, Neal folds the sweater neatly, then suddenly col-
lapses backward on the bed.*

Taw makes a startled move to help him but stops by the table.

NEAL

(Still flat) Then pack for me too.

TAW

Is that your answer?

NEAL

(Sits upright) It just may be.

TAW

(Sits at the table) No *may*-bes now.

NEAL

Then no, I haven't answered.

TAW

If I pack us both, we'll be gone for good. We'd leave here tonight—go someplace and breathe.

NEAL

(Takes a long breath) I'm not short of air.

TAW

We're strangling, Neal.

NEAL

Who's twisting *your* rope?

TAW

Our rope—you know well as me.

NEAL

Mother.

TAW

She's half.

NEAL

Not Porter.

TAW

Porter Farwell.

NEAL

(Waits, then firmly) I can't stop knowing my oldest best friend.

TAW

That's part of what every marriage is for—bury your dead and make a clean start. You love too many people.

NEAL

That's easy enough for an orphan to say.

TAW

Shame and you know it—I'd walk through streaming lava right now for my Aunt Jess.

NEAL

That's where we're going?—Hawaii? Fresh lava?

TAW

(Refuses the bait) Don't talk that trash—you know what I mean. But you come first, a long way first.

NEAL

You do for me, from the time I saw you.

TAW

That day at the horseshoe match, when you won?

NEAL

(Stands, goes to the window and faces out) I saw you maybe two months before that.

TAW

Never told *me*.

NEAL

A lot I never told you, maybe never will. *(Waits)* But I sure God saw you, naked as a peeled pear, drying your arm—among other parts.

TAW

Don't tell that lie.

NEAL

I climbed a tree to see you—nearly broke my neck.

TAW

(Smiles) Must have been the day Miss Ella washed the curtains. She told me not to bathe. *(Waits)* I hope you were alone.

NEAL

(Nods) Creeping home alone. Saw the top of Miss Taw Sefton's head and took the dare.

TAW

It can't have been worth it.

NEAL

(Smiles) I'll know someday. Right now I've just got a picture in my mind—you upright in that foggy bathroom with no other pair of hands to take and keep you. I thought I'd volunteer.

TAW

You waited long months.

NEAL

You weren't on the run.

TAW

Some other Peeping Tom could have beat you to me.

NEAL

I figured I'd win.

TAW

Stuck-up—think you did?

NEAL

Till this morning, yes.

TAW

And now you've lost?

NEAL

(Moves from the window halfway to Taw) I may have, yes.

TAW

(Rises in place at the table) I hope not.

NEAL

I believe you. *(Moves toward the door and opens it slowly)*

TAW

Take till tonight—

Neal faces her intently but does not speak or give a sign.

TAW

You want me to wait?

NEAL

(Calm but firm) You've decided everything else here today.

Taw moves a step toward him.

But Neal turns and leaves.

5

One-thirty in the afternoon. Porter sits at a table in the Downtown Cafe, finishing lunch.
    Neal enters, locates Porter and joins him.

PORTER

It's getting late. I started without you. Any change to report?

NEAL

(Waits) Let's leave that alone—my brain is *fried*.

Porter nods and watches Neal closely.

NEAL

(Waits) I guess I ought to just bunk at Mother's till Taw calms down, but with you up there—

PORTER

Neal, understand this—I'm not determined to live at your mother's; she and I are not some secret team out to drive you off.

NEAL

(Nods) I didn't think so.

PORTER

But if you're hunting space, it is a big house. I'll move out of your room the instant you want it. With ten minutes' notice, we can move me downstairs.

NEAL

The sewing room?

PORTER

I'm a pretty fair seamster.

NEAL

Those models of Mother's bust through the years wouldn't rile your sleep?

PORTER

Take more than any lady's bosom to wake me, tired as I am today.

NEAL

Don't worry about it, tonight anyhow. If I sleep at Mother's, I'll flop on the sofa till my plans congeal. Anything worth eating?

PORTER

(Glancing at the plate) Chicken dumplings, green peas and biscuits. They've got fish too. You need to eat.

NEAL

I doubt I'm hungry. Hell, I don't know *anything* I want.

PORTER

(Waits and then, in full awareness of the dare he takes, leans forward) I know what *I* want, every day from now on.

NEAL

Is it something I should hear?

PORTER

(Halting, the first confession of his life) I figured you knew, had known all your life. Some version of last night—a dugout, a river, deep night, you asleep.

NEAL

You awake, on guard?

PORTER

(Sits back, laughs, finds his answer slowly) Something like that. Crazy. And practical as—snowshoes—in August—in Mexico.

NEAL

I think they have mountains in Mexico where snow never melts.

PORTER

Hope they do. But this is Carolina. People go barefoot eight months a year.

NEAL

And stand stock-still in place all their lives. *(Waits)* Unless there's a war.

PORTER

After 1918, a *world* war's out. And the South won't rise.

NEAL

You don't know that; you read it somewhere. There's millions of square miles we've never seen. You and I've traveled more than anybody near; and where have we been?—north to Richmond, east to Nags Head, west far as Windy, no farther south than Charleston.

PORTER

I'm no big explorer.

NEAL

But you're miserable here.

PORTER

Not me, no.

NEAL

You had me fooled. I thought that was liquor you poured down your gullet. You drink more than me.

PORTER

I drink *with* you. You've begged me to.

NEAL

That's a pitiful reason.

PORTER

It's mine. I like it.

NEAL

Shame *on* you then.

PORTER

All right.

NEAL

(Waits) No wonder we're stuck; we've just been too damned lazy to run.

PORTER

You forgot your feet.

NEAL

Sir?

PORTER

Your two flat feet. Armageddon could come; you'd never get drafted, not with those feet.

NEAL

Forget my feet. I own four horses. And the car's been invented—we could head on south. We've never seen Texas. Hell, a Model A can drive in Spanish as fast as English.

PORTER

Faster. *(Waits)* When we get there—what? We can't *work* in Spanish.

NEAL

You're rich; you're the one with the big nest egg.

PORTER

Big enough to see us far as Social Circle, Georgia and buy us one fried-oyster dinner apiece.

NEAL

(Serious) I may want that.

PORTER

From now on out? Till Hell comes calling?

NEAL

(Waits) I'm too tired to choose, at least right now.

PORTER

Now's what you've got, to choose Taw at least. Me and Mexico or down on the river might wait awhile longer.

NEAL

(Calm) For me? All my life?

PORTER

I've answered that, Neal—most days you've known me.

NEAL

(Watches Porter, then firmly) Every livelong day.

Porter sits a moment, facing Neal; then stands in place and consults his pocket watch.

PORTER

Late here, boy. May lose my job.

NEAL

(Stands, serious) I'll speak to the boss.

Porter hurries out.

6

Immediately after. As Porter leaves, Neal turns back slowly, moves far downstage and faces the audience. As he speaks he gradually retreats; by the end he is far upstage, marooned.

NEAL

One thing I know I'm not is conceited. So believe what I say, in this one respect. The trouble, my whole life, has been this— people fall for me, what they *think* is me. They mostly call it love, and it generally seems to give them fits. They think life can't go on without me—when I know life can go on in the dark if they blind you, butcher you down to a torso, stake you flat on a rank wet floor and leave you lonesome as the last good soul.

Neal Avery can't save the *shrubbery* from pain, much less human beings. It may be the reason I act so bad to Taw and my mother and Porter, my friend. It may be why I'm soaked to the ears so much of the time—*I know I'm me,* an average white boy with all his teeth, not Woodrow Wilson or Baby Jesus or Dr. Pasteur curing rabies with shots.

Who on God's round Earth do they think I am? Who would patch their hearts up and ease their pain? If I stand still here for many years more, won't they wear me away like the Sphinx or a doorsill, just with the looks from their famished eyes?

If I wasn't a Methodist, if this wasn't home, wouldn't I be well advised to strip and run for the nearest desert cave and live among wolves or crows or doves? Wouldn't they simply elect me gamekeeper?

Am I ruined past help? Could I take ten steps on my own— here to there—much less flee for life, for my good and theirs?

7

Two in the afternoon, Roma Avery's kitchen. Roma is napping in a large rocker, a thick book open facedown in her lap.

Taw climbs the steps to the front door and knocks.

Roma wakes, frowning, and slowly moves to answer. At the sight of Taw, Roma waits in silence, smiling.

TAW

I know it's your nap time.

ROMA

(Still smiling) Wrong, Mrs. Avery. I seldom bat an eye—*(Waves Taw in)* Just pause once a day to think great thoughts. You must be collecting for a desperate cause.

TAW

Why's that?

ROMA

To call on me, alone, here in daylight. Who are the starving
Armenians this time?

TAW

The Averys.

ROMA

Not *this* Avery. I ate two drumsticks for lunch and peach
cobbler.

TAW

I haven't had a morsel since yesterday.

ROMA

Sit down. I'll tend to that.

TAW

I came for something else.

ROMA

(A long wait) Sit anyhow and tell me.

Roma returns to her chair, takes her book up and sits again.

Taw goes to an opposite chair but stands beside it.

Roma holds up the book.

ROMA

Read this yet?

TAW

No ma'm. I—

ROMA

You better! It's had me stroking my knee all week. Anything'll
make me touch this body is bound to be good.

TAW

Your body's all right, Mrs. Avery.

ROMA

For glue. Some days I think I'll walk myself, while I still have
steam and can see the road, to the nearest glue factory.

TAW

(Smiles) Wait a few years.

ROMA

You speaking for yourself or Neal or who?

TAW

Oh, the general populace. You know—most of us.

ROMA

Sit down please. You're lying. You never liked me.

Taw, to her own surprise, sits. With unusual care she settles her skirt and jacket.

TAW

Yes ma'm, I did—once or twice, when your rough edge showed.

ROMA

Like now?

Taw extends a hand as if to halt a charge.

Roma waits, then nods.

TAW

I didn't come here to fight.

ROMA

All right if you did.

TAW

I wouldn't know how.

ROMA

The hell you wouldn't. You took my one child off and broke him.

Though she nearly conceals it, Taw is stunned. No one else has struck as hard as this.

Roma searches Taw's face, then continues in the same level voice.

ROMA

I'm sorry. I'm cursed with telling the truth. Neal's father used to say "Roma, trouble with you is, you're a *truth* monger."

TAW

Neal told me that.

ROMA

It's nothing I'm proud of.

TAW

(Nods) I wondered.

ROMA

Last thing people want, especially your kin.

TAW

I want it now. *(Waits)* How have I broken Neal?

ROMA

You married him.

TAW

That was his idea as much as mine.

ROMA

More so, I'm sure—men invented mistakes. That didn't mean you had to compound it by climbing aboard, all smiles in bushels of satin and veil. Neal was smothered by the time the last note sounded.

TAW

Mrs. Avery, marriage is the way people live.

ROMA

Some few do, yes—the saints of the Earth. It fells most others in a few quick weeks, right dead in their tracks—still grinning like dogs from the wedding reception.

TAW

Then what are people meant to do about love?

ROMA

(Smiles) Ah *love.* Comes in more than one color and size.

People want their knees, and elsewhere, stroked—every week
or so. No problem with that; just ask somebody and pull down
the shades. Or your neighbors and God—keep fresh cakes
handy, visit the sick and send up thankful prayers once a day. I
pray at dawn; I'm more thankful then.

TAW

Don't mock me please.

ROMA

I'm not. Sit back. I haven't got to you.

TAW

I need to get home.

ROMA

You *do*. But I'll just take another minute. *(Waits) Love.* You and
Neal. The smoky kind—two months of fire, a year of coals,
decades of smoke. You've either got to stand still and learn to
breathe smoke or leave here alone, get your hands red with
scandal and hope to live it down.

TAW

Or leave here tonight—Neal and I both, just the clothes on our
backs. Leave you and Porter and the pitiful job, this dreadful
house—and watch the smoke clear, all on its own.

ROMA

(Not visibly fazed) Speak for you, Taw—*you.* Neal Avery lives
here. *(Leans forward slowly and points to the floor)*

TAW

I believe you.

ROMA

Blow me down!

TAW

I believe Neal dreams he still lives here. I'm finally asking you
to help me wake him up.

ROMA

And that means telling him goodbye forever and crouching up
here to die alone?

TAW

You're a young strong woman.

ROMA

Strong enough to fight.

TAW

And nobody ever leaves anyone *forever*, not their mother at
least.

ROMA

(Smiles, shakes her head) No ma'm, every day. Don't you know
that's the founding faith of America?—leave your poor old
mother in her cold sod hut and strike out with some pretty
thing for freedom: Ellis Island—Oklahoma.

TAW

(Waits) I've asked Neal to leave, with me—to anywhere.

ROMA

What's his answer?

TAW

None yet. He's got till tonight.

ROMA

To tell you whether he'll leave or not?

TAW

And stop drinking liquor with Porter Farwell till he drops in
ditches.

ROMA

(Smiles) You packed?

TAW

Yes.

ROMA

For you *and* Neal?

TAW

Just me, till tonight.

ROMA

What happens tonight?

TAW

Neal tells me his plan.

ROMA

Neal can't plan tying his shoes and you know it.

TAW

(Nods) He's learning right now. He's got till dark.

ROMA

(Laughs) Dark in what century—the twenty-third?

TAW

No ma'm. Now. He knows I won't wait.

ROMA

You said you could. I sat in church in a fine lace dress and heard you vow—cost me thirty-five dollars and it's hot as Bombay. I won't haul that out, ever again. You and Neal are *stuck*.

TAW

Not me, not for long. If Neal won't honor the vows we took, then he sets me free.

ROMA

You believe in freedom, this side of the grave?

TAW

I have to, yes.

ROMA

You think you've ever seen it? Show me a sample.

TAW

(Waits, then slowly shakes her head) You'd sit here and mock it.

ROMA

I'd weep for joy. I've waited long years.

TAW

I hope Neal and I can end your vigil.

ROMA

How so?

TAW

With a serious life together, wherever we go. Real love is freedom—two people free to choose but choosing each other, day by day.

ROMA

God help you, child.

TAW

He already has. He's guiding me now.

ROMA

(Studies her, bemused) I can't see the halo.

TAW

I prayed all night.

Roma thinks through that, rises in place and again studies Taw's face carefully, then extends her right hand.

ROMA

Then you don't need me. *(Waits)* Goodbye, Taw. I can wish you good luck.

Taw sits on a moment, then realizes she has been dismissed. She rises but declines to take Roma's hand.

TAW

You don't want to help?

ROMA

I think I have—all I honestly can. I can't improve on your plans and God's. *(Waits)* You need any cash?

TAW

No ma'm. I'm kin to some openhanded people.

ROMA

Your aunt in Raleigh?

TAW

Many more, many places.

ROMA

Then you'll be wanting to head on to them. *(Moves past Taw toward the door again, opens it, stands there waiting with a smile)*

Taw is incredulous but keeps her face steady. With no touch or wave, she moves past Roma and out of the house.

ACT TWO

1

The same day, three in the afternoon. Genevieve Slappy, still in her house-robe, works at a large sewing machine in her front room. Materials are strewn about her; she is plainly adept and proceeds intently for a moment. At the end of her seam, she faces the audience.

GENEVIEVE

I'm the youngest property-owner I know—this whole house is mine. Mother left it to me when my brother Dillard and his big family were jammed in a one-story matchbox on the hot side of town. She hoped I would sit here, quiet—renting rooms the rest of my life—and forget Wayne Watkins and the dream of marriage.

I don't understand. She and my father were happy together as any two ducks on a deep warm pond. Many times as a child I woke in the night and heard them laughing in the dark down the hall. But when my father died, Mother—young as she was—just started shrinking day by day till the night she vanished.

Or so I recall it. She never warned me off men or low-rated love till the evening she left us. Then that night, in the back bedroom, I took in her supper; and she said "Sit still while I tell you what's true." I sat by her knees, and she said "Stop waiting by the door like a dog." I said "Beg your pardon?" She shut her eyes and waited and then said "I'll pardon you when you can stand alone."

I'd been walking unaided from the age of ten months—it bowed my knees slightly—and I reminded her of that. I also mentioned how she'd leaned on Papa those twenty-eight good years. She didn't give an inch but turned her face to the wall, the picture she'd painted as a girl—of buffalo—and she said "Then I can't pardon you tonight, can I?"

I laughed "No ma'm. Wait till breakfast tomorrow." And she died before day—leaving me all this, as I said: *(Gestures around)* my life. So she hoped anyhow. She may yet prevail.

It *is* a strong house—heartwood beams and floors.

2

Immediately after, Genevieve continues sewing and does not hear Taw's first knock; but at the second knock, she goes, opens quickly, leads Taw to a littered daybed and motions her down.

TAW

You're busy.

GENEVIEVE

On my world-famed trousseau. Believe me, it can wait.

Taw sits.

Genevieve returns to her sewing chair.

TAW

You were right.

GENEVIEVE

She turned you down?

TAW

And tore me up.

GENEVIEVE

By telling the facts? She's noted for that. You heard what she did when Neal's father died?

TAW

No.

GENEVIEVE

Child, that was all but *radio* news. *(Waits)* They brought Mr. Avery's corpse to the house in a grand walnut coffin, and everybody gathered that night after supper to pay their respects. Neal was on hand to greet them and sober as a yardstick. But Roma Avery was nowhere in sight.

Everybody knew of course that she and the corpse had barely said "Morning" since Neal was born; so they hung on, hoping she'd finally appear in widow's weeds and some kind of tears. At nine P.M. Roma stalked in in pumps, a teal-blue dress, one strand of pearls and a *serious* screwdriver.

TAW

I won't ask why.

GENEVIEVE

Nobody else did. Miss Roma always explains herself. Straight as a rail, she went to the coffin and unscrewed the little brass plaque on the side. Next she turned to us all, held out the plaque and read the only two words — *At Rest.* Then she said " '*At Rest*'? If any son of a bitch was ever frying in Hell, it's Britt Butler Avery." *(Waits)* That cleared the mourners in four seconds flat.

TAW

(Smiles) I didn't stay many minutes longer today.

GENEVIEVE

But you said your piece?

TAW

I told her I meant to take Neal off from here.

GENEVIEVE

You never told me one word about that. Take him where, for
what?

TAW

Anywhere they have jobs. To clear his slate. To keep us married, like you want us to be.

GENEVIEVE

I wish you'd told me before you saw Roma. I'd have saved you
the trip. She could no more visualize Neal going farther than
her voice can reach than you'd see yourself as a virgin martyr in
the jaws of lions.

TAW

I know that now.

GENEVIEVE

Hush. You don't. And she'll fight you every inch you take.
(Waits) Did Neal say he'd leave?

TAW

Neal hasn't said anything clear enough to hear.

GENEVIEVE

Had he talked to his mother anytime today?

TAW

She didn't let on.

GENEVIEVE

He's talked to Porter; you can bet on that.

TAW

I hope not. But you're bound to be right.

GENEVIEVE

Then go beg Porter to ease your way. *(As Taw shakes her head)*
Porter Farwell can tame Neal Avery out of trees. I've seen him
do it—out of literal *trees* in the pitch-black winter night and
Neal buck naked on the top branch, drunk, stealing mistletoe.
Neal used to strip a lot.

TAW

Genevieve, I'd gladly eat fire and die for Neal; but God on His chair can't force me to beg my life and my husband's from Porter Farwell.

GENEVIEVE

Nothing wrong with Porter.

TAW

That a gun wouldn't cure.

GENEVIEVE

Or a wife and ten children.

TAW

Which is roughly as likely as kittens from cows.

GENEVIEVE

Taw, Porter is kind. His head may be a little lost in the mist, but he'd give you the last drop of water on Earth.

TAW

And hold your husband in his other hand.

GENEVIEVE

(Nods) He's sworn to Neal.

TAW

In whose church please?

GENEVIEVE

Oh just in *life*, from the cradle up. They've known each other forever, barring four days — Porter's four days older. No other friend's meant as much to either one.

TAW

Friendships need to end in childhood, along with mumps and five-year diaries.

Genevieve moves to her sewing machine and sits. She carefully pedals a short burst of stitching. Then she faces Taw.

GENEVIEVE

I thought we were friends—that we helped each other with our glorious lives. But since we aren't, or so you claim, then I'm free now to say what I've thought about you all day—you are out of your mind.

Taw, I *live* for a few friends and one shaky boy—Wayne Watkins—that won't even ask for my hand. You sound like Roma Avery, chaining people to you and gnawing their bones.

TAW

You notice I'm alone though.

GENEVIEVE

Damned right—and may be alone from here on out. People in general aren't in it for the pain. If you want company—Neal's or mine or a bobcat's—you got to let up.

TAW

Starting how?

GENEVIEVE

If I tell you—and I *know*—I'll be wasting good air.

TAW

Maybe not. I may be scared.

GENEVIEVE

Good—it's way past time. Listen. Roma turned you down. She'll never change course; and she'll have Neal up at her house right now, laying down her law and cutting at you. You need to find Porter—tell him truly what's happened and beg him to help you save your life, if you want this life.

TAW

(Stands and slowly moves toward the door, then turns) I may not want it, if it's hard as this.

GENEVIEVE

It is. Any set of good eyes sees that by age five. *(Waits)* I'll help you pack or I'll wait here and pray. But really, I can't keep talking like this. It's ruining my whole outlook on life, and I don't want it ruined. I'm a loving soul with too much to face.

Taw nods and leaves.

Genevieve slowly returns to work.

3

Three forty-five in the afternoon. Porter Farwell steps from Avery's Clothing, where he and Neal work, into the back alley. There among wood packing crates, Taw is waiting for him. Porter is genuinely puzzled.

PORTER

Taw—Jake said it was you, but I barely believed him. Come on inside.

TAW

I can't see Neal.

PORTER

Neal's up at his mother's.

TAW

Please let me speak here.

PORTER

(Smiles) You giving me the Gettysburg Address or Washington's Farewell to the Infant Nation?

TAW

I'm asking you to help me and my husband.

PORTER

Neal—*that* husband?

TAW

I'm too tired to joke. I hoped you'd be.

PORTER

I seem to have got a second wind after lunch. *(Waits)* It was a long night.

TAW

Second wind is all I'm asking you for, for me and Neal both — or *first* wind truly. I'm not sure you ever gave us first wind.

PORTER

It wasn't mine to give. I gave the groom *away*, remember? You took over there.

TAW

You've had him most nights.

PORTER

(Smiles) Way less than half. Neal's old enough to vote.

TAW

That's the reason I'm in this back alley now, eating crow by the handful — to ask you to take your hat out of the ring. Stop running for Neal.

Porter moves to a packing crate, politely motions Taw to another, then seats himself carefully.

Taw remains standing.

PORTER

My little office with Neal is for life — private dogcatcher maybe or municipal joke.

TAW

Not *so*, Porter. There's no more future in you and Neal, sleeping drunk by the road, than in peace on Earth.

Porter thinks, then suddenly rises and moves toward Taw.

Taw holds her ground.

Porter goes back and sits.

Then at last Taw sits.

PORTER

You turned gypsy on us?

TAW

Sir?

PORTER

You foreseeing things?

TAW

It doesn't take a gypsy or a telescope, just a set of eyes that have watched the world.

PORTER

And you've watched long enough to see all friendships fade and die?

TAW

(Nods) I'm an orphan, Porter.

PORTER

That's a famous fact. You could do lecture tours—Little Taw in the Snow.

TAW

(Waits) I pity you—the life you'll have.

PORTER

You foresee that too?

TAW

Right to the end—a dark rented room, an old man lonesome as a rock in the sky.

PORTER

(Waits, then laughs) I'd better start taking more exercise. I'll need extra strength, just standing upright with no helping hand. You of course foresee strong arms under you?

TAW

If you let Neal loose.

PORTER

You can't think *I'm* what's holding Neal?

TAW

Who else is in sight?

PORTER

His mother, his mind—all it dreams to do.

TAW

Neal Avery's mind is promised to me. I've got the signed oath—most people call it a marriage certificate.

PORTER

(Smiles) I signed it too.

Taw looks puzzled.

PORTER

As best man. Remember? The best man's the witness.

TAW

Then the best man leaves. That's his last duty.

PORTER

Where does he go? *(Waits, then laughs)* What am I meant to do?

TAW

Tell Neal to leave town—now, with his wife.

PORTER

Using what for money?—he works right here.

TAW

We're both strong as bears.

PORTER

Not Neal.

TAW

Then me—*me*, Porter: I'm one strong soul. I'll work for us both.

PORTER

While Neal turns to putty.

TAW

In *my* hands, at least—his legal mate. No, Neal's meant to be far stronger than you guess. He needs to be more than a lovable smile. I know; I've lain down beside him enough. He's waiting to find his own path and walk.

PORTER

And you're his guide through the underbrush?

TAW

The one he chose.

PORTER

He told me he had till sundown to choose.

TAW

(Waits) He has. But now I've begged you to help. Want me to crawl on my knees right here? *(Half-starts to kneel)*

PORTER

(Stops her with a wave) You didn't really hear my question, Taw. What am *I* meant to do?

TAW

(Waits) Hunt you up your own grown life.

Porter thinks, laughs a short low note, then rises. He moves toward the door, then turns.

PORTER

You more or less ruined my afternoon, but leave—I'll do the little I can.

TAW

He'll listen to you.

PORTER

(Smiles) He never has yet. You never understood—Neal Avery knows what he wants and takes it. Neal Avery, drunk, is clearer than most Baptist preachers at dawn. *(Rises from the crate and, through the following, moves slowly toward the door)*

The night before he married you, Neal drove me out toward the river; and we somehow got lost—in country we'd known every day of our lives. So we left the car and struck out walking on the sandy road. Neal said he could smell water straight ahead. I told him he was crazy; we'd get lost deeper.

He said "Stay with me. This is my last exhibit." I said "What of?" And Neal said "Powers I'm losing tomorrow." I walked on beside him; and in maybe half an hour we were wading in river water, warm on our knees.

On the way back home—it was already day—I asked Neal why he was losing powers. He said "I thought I'd be a human for a while." I said "Then who have I known up till now?" And he said "Your guess is good as mine, but it's been grand fun."

TAW

(Gently) I ended his fun? Cost him his powers?

PORTER

He never said that.

TAW

You just did.

PORTER

I told you a story.

TAW

With a moral at the end.

PORTER

I stopped short of that.

TAW

Spell it out, Porter. You're the only one *knows*.

PORTER

Step back.

Taw takes a step back.

PORTER

Not from me—I meant Neal.

TAW

(Looks around quickly) I'm on Mars now. I can barely *see* Neal, he's so far off.

PORTER

(Shakes his head slowly) You're right at his throat.

TAW

It's where I belong—*(Waits to calm)* Keep talking please.

PORTER

You're the trained talker. *(But then he steps closer; Taw waits in place)* See, Neal needs help just to draw his next breath. He can't be by himself long enough to shave. But he never heard those marriage vows, never guessed they were laws. You've told him now but he needs more time.

TAW

He's had a long year.

PORTER

Not really. Believe me—he's had just today, since you struck him at dawn.

TAW

But *you* understood every vow we took, the instant we spoke.

PORTER

(Nods) I did—I'm sorry.

TAW

(Waits to comprehend his concession, then moves a short step closer) Now what?

PORTER

For who?

TAW

Neal and me, you, his mother.

PORTER

Let me just speak for Neal. This is Neal's home, Taw—pull him up, he'll die. All his roots are here, all the lights that show him he's thriving and useful. Give him air and ground-room; he may well grow.

TAW

He's no plant, Porter. I'm not a plant doctor. Prescribe for the
humans.

PORTER

(Waits) Same prescription — air and room. *(Slowly turns to the
door)* Of course Porter Farwell may land behind bars, practic-
ing medicine without a state license.

Taw stays in place but gives a small wave.

TAW

We could bail you out.

PORTER

Start saving-up now. *(Nods goodbye and opens the door)*

TAW

Thank you, hear?

Porter watches her calmly but neither moves nor speaks.

Taw waits a moment, then hurries away.

4

*Immediately after. Porter shuts the door, returns to the crates
and faces the audience.*

PORTER

In a town this size, everybody's known your family since the
Seven Years' War; so you have to live most of your life in code —
little signs and fables for the kind and wise, not actual touch or
plain true words. That's been all right by me most times; it
keeps you from having to make up your mind too fast, or ever.

For years you can walk around some strong magnet and
never ask why or be told to explain. Then when you least expect

it, somebody you've known from the dark of the womb will step up and reach for the trunk of your life and shake it like a cyclone, and you'll shed your apples in full public view.

It happened to me my first year in high school, fourteen years old—English class, of course. Miss Speed Brickhouse went round the room asking everybody what they hoped to be; and everybody answered some sensible way—storekeeper, bank teller, practical nurse. Then she called on me—"Porter, what's your plan?"

I was already helping at Avery's Store—Neal and I on Saturdays—and I figured I'd sell men's clothing for life. But what I said was what slipped out. To Miss Speed's withered face, and twenty-six children vicious as bats, I said "I hope to be a lighthouse for others."

Miss Speed tried to save the day by saying the church was the noblest career, but everybody knew she was wrong, and they *howled*—right on through Commencement three whole years later.

I found the strength to hold my ground though, and I never explained. I knew I'd found, and told, the truth—a real light, for safety, in cold high seas.

Not for *others* though; I lied in that—just for Neal Avery, the one I'd long since chosen as being in special need and worthy of care. I may well have failed.

5

Four o'clock in the afternoon. Roma Avery's kitchen. Roma is finishing icing a cake.

Neal enters briskly.

Roma comes from the counter with her cake and sets it at one end of the table.

Neal sits, looks toward the cake and touches it but does not taste his finger.

ROMA

Let me know when you're ready.

Neal nods but does not meet her eyes.

Roma sits at his left.

Finally Neal turns and studies her.

NEAL

You're in one piece—no obvious abrasions.

Roma looks puzzled.

NEAL

On the phone you sounded like enema-time at the St. Louis Zoo.

ROMA

When were you in St. Louis?

NEAL

In my dreams.

ROMA

Then maybe you and Taw can go there soon.

NEAL

Why so?

ROMA

Taw said you were leaving. She paid me a visit with that little news.

NEAL

News to me.

ROMA

Then your wife flat lied.

NEAL

Mother, Taw's failings don't include deceit. You misunderstood.

ROMA

Enlighten me please.

NEAL

Taw thinks this whole place is bad for me—her and me.

ROMA

Where would be good?

NEAL

Where she and I could be together more.

ROMA

What's stopping you from clamping your pink limbs together sixteen hours a day?

NEAL

(Laughs but waits, then not facing Roma) That'll be my private concern, please ma'm.

ROMA

You leaving here would concern *me* deeply. You're my right hand in business; you're my one blood child.

NEAL

Porter runs the store; I'm just the handshaker, the boy with the grin. And I'm not sure I ever volunteered to be your child.

ROMA

(Smiles) Of course you did. In Heaven little unborn babies are shown snapshots of lonely women; they're given plenty time to study each face. Then they choose who they like.

NEAL

And are stuck with the choice? *(Smiles)* Mother for life?

ROMA

Life and beyond. Does marriage offer that?

NEAL

Jesus said nobody gets married in Heaven.

ROMA

Which is why it's Heaven. But he didn't say people forget their mothers.

NEAL

Didn't say redheads get in half-price either.

Roma cuts a slice of cake, extends it to Neal.

Neal shakes his head No.

Roma sets the plate in the absolute center of the table before them.

ROMA

Leave tonight. I'll support you ninety days.

NEAL

Whoa—

ROMA

Asheville. Chattanooga. Hell, Salt Lake City.

NEAL

And you'll come behind us, to balance the books?

ROMA

(Smiles) I'll sit in this house and eat thin slices of my own strong heart till nobody's left still standing but me.

NEAL

After that?

ROMA

I'll join you in eternity, angel.

NEAL

(Laughs, reaches for the slice of cake and tastes it) I'll make you a serious proposition. *(Waits as Roma leans forward)* I shoot myself late tonight by the river. You bury me neatly in my pinstriped suit. Then, with no harsh word, you give Taw ten thousand dollars cash. She'll leave. Your path'll be clear. Taw can start over fresh.

ROMA

(Waits) Would she sign a paper?—no further claim on me?

NEAL

(Eats more cake) Take me seriously for once.

ROMA

I do. I accept your proposition.

NEAL

(Laughs) Want to oil the gun? You can hold it maybe. I can fire it with my toes.

ROMA

I'd have a long wait. *(When Neal looks puzzled)* You'd never do it. *(Waits)* You love the world.

NEAL

(Laughs) What makes you think that?

ROMA

Love it far more than I or your father. I've known it almost since you were born, when I realized everyone that saw you loved you. I was jealous at first—so few loved me—and then I saw the reason: no virtue of yours; you just loved the world; you begrudged it nothing. Your kind is so rare, people love you on sight.

NEAL

I can thank you, Mother, but say you're wrong. I'm just a regular no-count boy that won't be a man but wants a man's pay n good cook to curl up next to at night.

ROMA

Taw said there wasn't much curling up.

NEAL

(Smiles) Since I love the whole world, I can't be partial to any one creature.

ROMA

Don't leave here, Neal.

NEAL

They were busy at the store. I better get back.

ROMA

You know what I mean.

NEAL

No ma'm. But I know you'll spell it out for me right now—slowly, in English. *(Raises both hands as if to lead a band)*

ROMA

You leave and I'll die.

NEAL

I believe you.

ROMA

And you still mean to leave?

NEAL

I haven't said that.

ROMA

But you will, by dark.

NEAL

(Standing in place) You're the prophetess, Mother. I'm just the boy that loves here-and-now.

ROMA

Then I'm as here-and-now as anything else.

Neal moves to her, slowly leans to kiss the top of her head. Then he rises and stands still a moment before he leaves.

6

Immediately after. Roma stays at the table and faces the audience.

ROMA

Till the day he died, my father was the thing I thought loved me. He was young—nineteen the year I was born—and he seldom spoke ten words a day; so he never *told* me, never spoke the word: not *love*, not in my hearing at least. That was fine by me. All this talk of mine—my Famous Fountain of Truth— came after he died.

Till I was four I said not a word and almost never cried, and by then Mother'd told the world I was mute. Father didn't seem to worry a bit but rode me everywhere he went, on his broad English saddle, far out in the country—he managed timber for his great-grandfather, who'd known James Madison when he was a boy.

The winter I was four, we were out near the river, in a noon so bright my eyes stayed shut; and Father spoke for the first time in hours. He said "Rome, speak now—this precious instant—or nevermore."

So my eyes clicked open, and I said plainly "Let's just keep going on from here." I meant *Not home. Anywhere else but home*, though Mother was a saint almost beyond doubt.

Father said not a word but spurred us on. I think he obeyed me, I honestly do, till midafternoon. At least we saw trees we'd never passed before, both of us silent as stones, each step.

Then a moment came when I felt him turn back. I knew because I was happy till then; but once that horse turned home at a jog, I broke like a stick—for good, for life. Just two nights later Father died across town at a girl's back door, shot once by her brother in the midst of his heart in dark thick as fur.

Next morning I commenced normal speech, no tears, with nobody I much cared to address—not then or since. In the last twenty years, I've enjoyed Neal of course. Father shows in his eyes sometimes, in the dusk. *(Slowly strokes her eyes)*

7

Four-thirty in the afternoon, Avery's Clothing. Porter, with a tape measure round his neck, sorts trousers on a table. Another table, bare, is nearby.

Neal enters.

PORTER

You seem to be alive —

Neal extends his arms, then his legs, as if to check them.

NEAL

Barely, I guess.

PORTER

And you calmed your mother?

NEAL

Jesus, with morphine, wouldn't calm Mother. Taw paid her a visit.

PORTER

Taw's had a full day. She honored *me.*

NEAL

When?

PORTER

Just now, in the alley. She wouldn't come in.

NEAL

(Sits on the bare table) What did she want?

PORTER

Perfect peace, perfect light.

NEAL

Porter, tell the truth.

PORTER

Swear to God. I just changed the wording. *(Waits)* She wants me to beg you to do her will.

NEAL

You promise you would?

PORTER

I think so, yes.

NEAL

(Waits, then harshly) Go to it. Beg.

PORTER

Keep your word to Taw.

NEAL

Recite me the vows.

PORTER

Sir?

NEAL

The marriage vows—you were there by me, weren't you?

PORTER

(Smiles) "Till death do us part."

NEAL

Then what about Mexico—high snow in August?

PORTER

Take her there, sure. She's earned the view.

NEAL

It was our idea—yours and mine: today, off and on for years. You backing out now?

PORTER

It was no idea—just our latest hangover. I sell britches, Neal, and gloves and socks. I will till I die. You and I've got the future of a keg of drowned cats.

NEAL

You always said that friendship outlasted women and rocks.

PORTER

I doubt it now.

NEAL

Since Taw's little visit?

PORTER

Since the day you saw her by the horseshoe pit.

NEAL

I won the match, Porter. Taw didn't stop me. No girl ever has. I can look and still throw.

PORTER

You weren't just looking that day; I saw you.

NEAL

I was also eating six brown-sugar pies and winning a sack race—you see that too?

PORTER

(Nods) And drinking two full jars of raw apple brandy. But Taw Sefton changed you for good, at first sight.

NEAL

I thought she looked good; I could tell she was smart.

PORTER

You thought she was God, with an angel squad.

NEAL

Get serious.

PORTER

Previous times I'd watched you skate fast figures round two dozen girls and plow home at daybreak, not even fazed. But Taw struck you like a pig-iron truck. When I drove you home, you were still burning high.

NEAL

She did look fine. And she talked plain sense, with no mean edge. Seemed not to think I was any big savior.

PORTER

She *chose* you, Neal. I watched her do it.

NEAL

She gave me two minutes—she was with Tim Page.

PORTER

That was all she needed. She knew on the spot. Tim Page might as well have been in Cuba.

NEAL

It did move fast. *(Waits)* Now we're *stopped*—hell, pasted on the windshield.

PORTER

Crank it, boy. It's your vehicle and you're at the wheel. But slower this time.

NEAL

(Waits) Climb back in.

PORTER

Sir?

NEAL

You. I need you. Let's clear out. Now.

PORTER

For how long?

NEAL

A few days. Ten years.

PORTER

With Taw in the middle?

NEAL

She'd go her own way.

PORTER

Your mother would too, straight to the Law. We'd come back in irons—embezzler's jail.

NEAL

Tell me one thing plain—you don't want to go anywhere but here?

PORTER

No I don't.

Neal waits, then stands and takes three steps to leave.

PORTER

Neal, God and you know I'd go with you to Asia—on yak-back—through—hail—if there seemed any chance we'd end up glad.

NEAL

We'd be taking a *trip;* the sky wouldn't fall.

PORTER

On me it would. Dumb old me. See, everything I know lives here. I might not know how to breathe elsewhere.

NEAL

(Points to his eyes) Keep trusting *me.* I'll teach you to breathe and far more, friend—all grades of wonders. *(Waits)* We'll be free, Lord Jesus!

PORTER

No, I'm Porter Farwell—always will be.

NEAL

You'd be Porter *free.*

PORTER

(Waits) I'm free right now, of all but you.

NEAL

(Waits in place, facing Porter frankly) Wasn't that a choice?

PORTER

(Nods) Made by me.

NEAL

Then I can't help you, can I?

PORTER

(Waits) Yes. Go to Taw—by dark. Soon now.

Neal shakes his head slowly—refusal? disbelief?—and leaves.

Porter takes his tape measure and carefully calculates the length of his left arm.

8

Six-thirty in the evening, Taw and Neal's room. Taw is setting two places at the center table; and behind on the stove, supper is cooking. She has changed into her newest dress, severe but becoming. At the foot of the bed, her two suitcases stand packed and ready.

Genevieve, bearing a large dish, knocks.

Taw balks before answering.

Genevieve opens the unlocked door.

GENEVIEVE

I'm not Neal Avery but I *can* cook beans. These are navy beans; they can sail you to Spain.

TAW

I may not need to go farther than Raleigh but thank you, Gen.

Genevieve moves to the oven, puts in the beans.

Taw continues table-setting.

GENEVIEVE

I see you're expecting a guest anyhow.

TAW

Is my husband a guest? *(Smiles)* Well yes, I'm setting the table on faith. And cooking enough for the Elks' Lodge banquet.

GENEVIEVE

(Moves toward the door) Call me if you need another mouth to help eat. I'll be upstairs praying.

TAW

For what?

GENEVIEVE

You and Neal, me and Wayne, all lonely souls.

TAW

Wayne's not dropping by?

GENEVIEVE

It's the night he cuts his daddy's hair; that can take several days.

TAW

The old fellow's bald.

GENEVIEVE

No, that's his step-dad; his real dad's shaggy as a cold Shetland pony. *(Opens the door)*

TAW

Please sit down.

GENEVIEVE

I'd be in the way.

TAW

I'm not too sure there *is* a way.

GENEVIEVE

Play like there is. That's my big philosophy; it got me this far.

Again Taw beckons her to come back and sit.

Genevieve goes to the chair.

TAW

I'm a terrible truster. If your parents die on you—

GENEVIEVE

(Her hand in the air, a brake on Taw) Don't tell me again; I'm scared enough.

TAW

You'll be all right; both of us will.

GENEVIEVE

People die every day, flat howling lonesome.

TAW

There are far worse things than a lone life.

GENEVIEVE

Name one.

TAW

(Waits) Watching children starve.

GENEVIEVE

Or letting go of a child good as Neal. *(Points)* I see those bags.

TAW

I'm packed to leave if Neal says leave—with him or alone. I'm ready for supper if that's the plan. You and Porter both said *Let go.*

GENEVIEVE

You truly saw Porter? I bet *he* was kind.

TAW

He said *Let go,* the same as you.

GENEVIEVE

(Shakes her head No) I said start trying to like Neal's nature, the one God gave—

TAW

Porter said I might hold him if I just surrendered. I never once thought I had any guns.

GENEVIEVE

You're armed all right.

TAW

I guess I can try to blind my eyes to some of his ways. But what I suspect is, the *sight* of me hurts him—just me in this room where he comes to rest.

GENEVIEVE

Wayne thinks I'm a damned federal marshal with bloodhounds, handcuffs and convict stripes. But I'll wait him out. One day he'll wake up and see I'm the person that loves his eyes and how he walks and will be true to him in any dark corner.

TAW

You've killed your pride. Mine is still so strong I can barely bend down.

GENEVIEVE

Pride's a sin, in all churches, Taw. Course I never had much. I *wait* a lot and it ruins my posture—I slouch through fights.

TAW

Not I. *(Extends both arms)* I'm covered with mine and Neal's scars.

GENEVIEVE

(Actually looks at both Taw's arms) Yours don't show.

TAW

I know where they are. I can't forget—

GENEVIEVE

Forget. *Now.* Catch a case of amnesia. Enter life fresh as a rose, this instant.

TAW

(Smiles) A rose with the blight—

GENEVIEVE

The world loves a rose.

Neal has approached. Now he knocks at the door.

Genevieve looks to Taw, mouths the name Neal and rises to leave.

Taw firmly motions her down, then goes and opens the door.

Neal is empty-handed.

TAW

Lost your key? It was open anyhow.

NEAL

I thought I'd play the gent for once.

TAW

I'll remember you that way then—many thanks. *(Gestures him in)*

NEAL

You're certain now?

TAW

It's where we can talk till the rent expires. The landlady's here—

GENEVIEVE

(Rising) And outward bound.

NEAL

(Gravely) Sit down, stay still, I brought you a message.

Neal moves toward Genevieve, searching his pockets.

Genevieve looks increasingly anxious.

Finally Neal throws up his hands in failure.

NEAL

It was nothing but a wire.

GENEVIEVE

A *wire?* Who's dead?

NEAL

From Wayne.

GENEVIEVE

Wayne?

NEAL

You're developing a problem with your eardrums, Gen. I said "From Wayne"—your aging beau. As I passed Western Union just now, they asked me to bring it; tipped me ten cents—here. *(Reaches for a dime and hands it to Genevieve)*

GENEVIEVE

(Slaps his arm aside) Neal, you owe me a whole world more than a thin silver dime. Where is Wayne and what in God's name does he say?

NEAL

You assume I took the liberty of reading a private dispatch?

GENEVIEVE

Wires are public property. How far has he gone? Is he under arrest?

NEAL

(Removes the wire from an inside pocket, opens it slowly and reads precisely) "Wheeling, West Virginia, 1:30 P.M." *(Waits)* "Up here suddenly with Dad and Dave. Will you marry me Friday if I get home safe? Yours cordially, Wayne." *(Hands over the wire)*

GENEVIEVE

(Studies it well, then crushes it in her palm) Cordially? They're bound to be drunk.

TAW

Who is Dave?

GENEVIEVE

Mr. Watkins' dog—the one that can sing.

TAW

I hope he can drive; those mountain roads are instant death.

GENEVIEVE

Of course they are. What else would Fate hold for Genevieve Slappy?

NEAL

Shall we join in prayer?

GENEVIEVE

No. *(Waits)* Neal, is one single word of this true?

Neal silently raises his right hand—an oath.

GENEVIEVE

You somehow made this whole thing up. Taw, do you believe this fool?

TAW

Forging a wire's a federal offense.

GENEVIEVE

That never stopped Neal.

NEAL

Gen, trust your best friend. Step on upstairs; you'll get a surprise.

GENEVIEVE

(To Neal) I'm in serious pain. What's true in all this?

NEAL

What I just said. Go sit by your hearth; your reward's on the way.

GENEVIEVE

And it's not bad news?

NEAL

Not for you, no ma'm.

Genevieve stands and heads for the door; then looks back, incredulous.

NEAL

Have I ever lied to you?

GENEVIEVE

Just ten times a day since we met in first grade.

NEAL

I'm not lying now. Go in peace; live to thank me.

GENEVIEVE

(Opens the door) Taw, those beans should be warm by now.

TAW

Thank you, Gen. Keep me posted; I'll do the same.

GENEVIEVE

(Nods) Call the Law if I scream.

NEAL

Absolutely.

GENEVIEVE

Not you, fool. Taw, call the true *Law* if I yell murder.

TAW

(Raising her hand) Cross my heart.

Genevieve leaves.

Neal moves to lock the door.

TAW

Leave it unlocked please.

NEAL

You expecting somebody?

TAW

I guess not, no.

Neal turns the key, then walks to the table.

TAW

(Points to the ceiling) You didn't lie to her?

NEAL

I forged the wire but she'll be happy soon. *(As Taw frowns)* I saw Wayne buying a diamond just now, the size of a gnat—for sweet Genevieve. *(Waits)* May I rest my feet?

TAW

Help yourself. Sit down.

Taw moves to the stove and continues to work.

After he stands in the midst, seeming lost, Neal walks an uncertain path toward the Morris chair. He stands and regards it like a new-found place; then he seems to measure it with slow gestures. None of his actions is strained or comic; he has no sense of entertaining Taw. She is gone from his mind. Finally he sits, leans well back and shuts his eyes.

Taw goes on cooking, adjusting the table settings, pouring two glasses of cool water and setting them precisely by each of their places. Throughout she glances nervously at Neal till at last she cannot bear the silence.

TAW

Neal, are you eating here?

Neal makes a long deep sound—agreement?

Taw steps up behind the sofa, leans over; she wants to smile but cannot trust herself, not to mention trusting Neal.

TAW

Will I ever know?

NEAL

(Eyes still shut) If I ever get back.

The dreamy words half-startle Taw; she withdraws in silence and stands by the table.

TAW

From where; where are you?

NEAL

(Very slow and distant) Way out in what may just be a dream. Moving, moving—

TAW

(Quietly but with gathering force) Move gently. *(Waits)* Move, Neal. Come on.

NEAL

I'm flying, girl.

TAW

Your own private plane? *(Starts moving bowls of food to the table)*

NEAL

I think it's—sure: my private *arms.*

TAW

(Still stocking the table) You must be hungry—are you strong enough to make it? Can I guide you in?

Neal waits a long moment, then rolls to his left side, faces the audience and opens his eyes.

Throughout what follows, Taw moves between final adjust-
ments at the table and furtive trips to lean toward Neal and test
the truth or fiction of his dream.

NEAL

I'm ten years old. The other children hate me, and I start to
run. We're on a big ledge of a hill, steep sides. They're about to
catch me; they've grabbed my shirttail. But I run the last step
over the ledge and fall through space toward a sharp rock
valley. The children yell "We're sorry. Come back."

I wish I could; I always loved them. But I'm bound to die.
Then my arms stretch out on the wind rushing by. And—
God!—I rise fifty yards in a sweep before I level off and glide.
I'm scared cold-stiff but I flap my arms, and this time I
understand I've learned to fly.

The sun breaks out—there's been a lot of mist—and natural
as sleep, I'm climbing and banking and looping-the-loop
while all the cruel children line up on the ledge with their
mouths wide open and beg me to land and teach them how. I
just glide on. *(Shuts his eyes again, then slowly sits up, rubs his*
face)

TAW

(Stops at the table) I thought people loved you.

NEAL

They do, till they know me. Then *they* beg for wings.

TAW

Were you really asleep?

NEAL

Maybe. I wonder. I've dreamed that before, many times
through the years. How long was I out?

TAW

Less than three minutes. Maybe you were snoozing. *(Waits)*
The trip make you hungry?

NEAL

I think maybe so.

TAW

(Gestures to the food) It's here then, abundant.

NEAL

(Stands slowly) How much?

Through the following Neal never smiles or teases. He seems at least a half-new man in his gravity, his voice.

Taw is enveloped early in the change; a half-new woman begins to show in her, convinced of her power but generous-hearted.

TAW

Food for hundreds.

NEAL

(Shakes his head) How much, if I sit down and eat—how much do I pay?

TAW

You own it already. You well know that.

NEAL

(Still in place) Then you changed the deal.

TAW

Sir?

NEAL

Your morning deal—I would stop my old life and leave here with you.

TAW

I meant I wanted to love you, Neal—in your right mind and *present,* after sundown at least.

NEAL

That simple? Just that?

TAW

(Nods) Where I could see and reach you.

NEAL

I can see you plainly from here. *(Extends a hand as if to touch her, then lets it fall)*

TAW

Come two steps nearer.

NEAL

(Takes two large steps) See how I've changed?

TAW

(Studies his face) I'd never have known you.

NEAL

Notice the clear eyes, the firm trusty jaw?

TAW

(Nods) A whole new man.

NEAL

(Holds up a cautionary hand) A great deal is hid under these fine clothes.

TAW

And all of it changed?

NEAL

That's your gamble, the risk you take.

TAW

You too. Three-quarters of me is submerged.

NEAL

That sank the Titanic—the buried ice.

TAW

(Touches her chest) I doubt this is ice.

Neal comes farther toward her and reaches again—still a yard short.

NEAL

(Nods) Warm, from here.

Taw nods.

Neal waits, then takes the last steps and touches her chest lightly, just above her breasts.

NEAL

You win then? For now?

TAW

(Shakes her head No) I've lost more than you—for good, I suspect.

NEAL

(Covers her eyes) Don't look that far. I might be gone.

TAW

(Moves her face clear but stands in place) The *world* might, Neal—be ashes by midnight, you and me with it.

NEAL

Fine by me.

TAW

Not me.

NEAL

You're young.

TAW

I'm old as the moon—that tired at least.

NEAL

How tired is the moon?

Then a distant cry. From here to the end, a ritual slowing—no hint of farce.

Neal and Taw look to the ceiling.

GENEVIEVE'S VOICE

(Excited but entirely clear) Wayne, my darling! It's glorious—and Lord God, look, it fits! *(Waits)* The answer is Yes—any *day*, and forever.

Neal, unsmiling, looks down at Taw.

NEAL

Do we call the Law?

TAW

(Facing Neal and also grave) She never meant that—I'm all but
sure.

NEAL

You take the responsibility then?

TAW

(Waits) I do.

*Still calm and grave, Taw steps back slowly and gestures toward
supper.*

*Neal waits a moment, then moves to the table, pulls out Taw's
chair and seats her slowly. Then he moves to the opposite chair
and sits.*

Taw passes him a large white bowl.

Neal nods and accepts it.

NIGHT DANCE

September 1945

ACT ONE

1

Six o'clock in the evening. Taw Avery sits at a desk in the living room of her and Neal Avery's apartment — the entire bottom half of the home of their landlady, Genevieve Watkins. The sparse furnishings are part Victorian oak, part 1930s Grand Rapids modern. Taw is grading a high stack of student papers. Distant radio-music plays, popular songs of the Second War years.

The hall door opens slowly and Neal Avery enters. He is in his work suit, a light seersucker with a red necktie. He shuts the door, takes three steps in, then stops and waits. His body and face are plainly exhausted.

Taw finishes marking the paper before her.

NEAL

Give him an A.

TAW

It's a she and she's dumb as that door.

NEAL

(Looks back) This door's solid oak, Taw. Oak's strong and smart.

TAW

(Notes his exhaustion) You have a hard day?

NEAL

I guess it was light. All the back-to-school rush has petered out. *(Moves to a table and shuffles the mail)* How was yours?

TAW

A mess. Seems very likely our fine new principal's a secret souse.

NEAL

Mr. Rawls? He hasn't exposed himself in chapel like that last fool?

TAW

(Smiles) Not below the waist yet, but his breath'd kill mules. I had to take Wylie Coleman in today for his first paddling of the fall, and blessed if Mr. Rawls wasn't fast asleep! Keeps a cot in his office for what he claims is high *blood*-pressure.

NEAL

(Smiles) Don't tell on him. The world had trouble before it had liquor.

TAW

(Sings) "Seems to me I heard that song before." *(Sets her papers in order and dusts at the desk with a handkerchief)*

Neal moves forward, bends to Taw and kisses her neck. When he stands back, we see that his face is grim.

Taw accepts his attention but quickly stands and moves past him.

TAW

I'm late with supper—got hypnotized: geography tests. Ecuador, the gold of the Incas.

NEAL

We won't need supper.

TAW

(Studies his face) You sick, poor boy?

NEAL

Not really, no ma'm.

TAW

(Fans herself with a quick hand) It's hot as cinders. Open a window. *(When Neal stalls, she moves toward a window)*

NEAL

Taw, steady yourself. *(Takes a telegram from his pocket and opens it)* They brought this wire to the store just now, for Genevieve. *(Reads)* "The President regrets to inform you that your husband Sergeant Wayne T. Watkins was killed 6 September on Okinawa—" *(His voice breaks. He looks up to Taw; his face is wrenched)*

TAW

They surrendered weeks ago—

NEAL

The emperor did. But Japanese snipers are all out there. *(Gestures outside as though this were a South Pacific island)*

TAW

Is that in the wire?

NEAL

(Waits for composure) I may not have had the honor of serving the stars and stripes, but I read the paper.

TAW

Does Genevieve know?

NEAL

(Extends the telegram) They brought it straight to me at the store—two hours ago. Thought *we* should tell her.

TAW

Why did you wait?

NEAL

(At the hint of blame, he is firm) Taw, I knew Wayne from the month I was born. I had to get where I could face his wife.

TAW

Did that mean a drink?

NEAL

Give me *some* human credit. I loved a boy for years; he's gone. I never marched far as the city limits; Wayne went round the world and is dead for his pains.

TAW

You tried the Navy and they wouldn't have you.

NEAL

(Waits, then nods) I don't need memos from your big file.

TAW

You tried your best.

NEAL

Poor Wayne didn't. Wayne couldn't have shot a black bull in a bathtub.

TAW

Any chance this is just some awful mistake?

Neal is caught by the chance.

TAW

Call the Red Cross; they know everything.

NEAL

If Genevieve wants. It's her business now and you know Gen— she'll pole-axe over like a shed in a storm.

TAW

I bet she'll surprise you.

Taw moves back into the midst of the room, then drops on a hard straight chair as if struck. Her eyes shut tightly.

NEAL

Are you all right?

TAW

(Waits, then raises her head and nods) The truth just hit me.

NEAL

Truth's famous for that. Rest a minute, then we'll walk on up.

Neal moves toward her but she waves him back.

TAW

I'll go. She's up there now; hear the music?

NEAL

I knew her first.

TAW

(Waits, then shakes her head hard and stands) She'll just be ashamed if you see her in trouble.

While Neal thinks, Taw moves past him and stops at the door.

TAW

Start the rice for me; it's already washed. *(Opens the door and steps toward the hall)*

NEAL

Call if she needs me—

Taw nods and leaves.

Neal still holds the telegram. He folds it carefully, lays it on the desk, then moves toward the kitchen.

2

Immediately after. Genevieve's apartment, the upper half of the house. Genevieve sits on an overstuffed sofa, dealing solitaire on a new coffee table. Her radio plays softly in the background—Tommy Dorsey, "Boogie Woogie."
   Taw approaches and knocks firmly once.
   Genevieve plays a card.

GENEVIEVE

It's open; come in.

Taw opens slowly and stands in the door.

GENEVIEVE

Those tiny footsteps! Girl, you're losing weight; *I'm* losing this game.

Taw stands in place.

Genevieve deals more cards and stumbles on luck — in a long last rush, she wins the game. Then she rises, smiling.

GENEVIEVE

I knew I'd win — been happy all day. Got my wig washed and set. *(Tugs at her real hair)* Let's celebrate.

TAW

(Smiles and moves forward) You look good. Sure.

Genevieve leaves for the kitchen.

Taw goes to a framed photograph of Wayne, studies it while she hears Genevieve's clatter from the kitchen, then quickly puts it down.

Genevieve returns with two bottles of beer, motions Taw to a chair and returns to the sofa. They both drink.

TAW

I've never been partial to beer but it's cold.

GENEVIEVE

(Points to the radio) I'm partial to that *piece* they're playing. Wayne'll die when he sees I bought a Victrola. But I worked for it, and it's his welcome-home. We can dance all night.

Taw shakes her head slowly and tries to speak.

GENEVIEVE

Stuck-up. I know it's not Chopin, but it lights *my* fire. *(Boogies in place, both arms in the air; then stops, facing Taw)*

TAW

Wayne's dead, Genevieve.

Genevieve's arms wave on a moment, then fall. She goes entirely still and watches Taw closely.

GENEVIEVE

What a thing to say. I been good to you.

TAW

Better than any soul left alive. But I'm sorry—it's true.

GENEVIEVE

The damned war's over. I heard from Wayne Tuesday. *(Points east)* He's eating chow·mein right now in Okinawa.

TAW

(Shakes her head slowly) He's on Okinawa but he's bound back now. Neal just got the wire.

GENEVIEVE

Neal? Neal has finally gone too far. *(Rises quickly)* I'll tell him myself.

TAW

Stop. *(Motions her down)* It's the pure-God truth. They sent it up here by Neal, to spare you.

GENEVIEVE

(Stands a moment, then carefully sits) Jesus, if this is your idea of mercy, push my front teeth in—I'd enjoy it more.

TAW

Gen, there's no kind way. Wayne was shot by a sniper. The President signed the telegram.

GENEVIEVE

Harry Truman can't write his own name—

TAW

He knows the facts.

GENEVIEVE

(Still watching Taw intently) Say we're both asleep.

TAW

I've never been wider awake in my life.

GENEVIEVE

God wouldn't do this to me now, Taw. Wayne lived through the whole war, slow as he is.

TAW

Neal can call up the Red Cross tonight. But for now, it's the truth.

Genevieve rises and moves to a window.

Taw stands in place.

GENEVIEVE

(Looking out the window) What do I do?

TAW

Maybe go tell his father.

GENEVIEVE

He never liked me.

TAW

Then come downstairs and help me cook supper.

GENEVIEVE

I couldn't eat a mouthful.

TAW

Don't stay here, Gen. The worst hasn't come.

GENEVIEVE

(Finally facing Taw, hotly) You're running over with kindness tonight. The worst! Name one thing worse than this.

TAW

—The moment the shock wears off and you *know.* You can't howl to bare walls; don't stay alone.

GENEVIEVE

(Calming as she speaks) I stayed here alone when my mother died. I stayed here alone for six dry years while Wayne made up his mind to love me—I'd sit up here and sing to the wallpaper, no other ears. I can tell you now the number of

boards in this *floor*—I counted them daily, right here, flat-alone. I guess I can manage a few more hours.

TAW

Don't. I need you. I was fond of Wayne.

GENEVIEVE

(Waits to think that carefully through) He loved your eyes. He said you could see things a cat would miss.

TAW

I can. I can see I need you now. *(Smiles shyly and offers her hand in the air)*

Genevieve waits, then slowly moves toward her.

3

Immediately after, the Averys' apartment. Taw opens the hall door and motions Genevieve to enter first.
Genevieve obeys, takes three short steps and halts inside. Taw moves on around her.

TAW

(Gently) Neal?

No immediate answer, then Neal appears in the kitchen door, dish towel in hand.

NEAL

(Faces Genevieve, waits) I've loved you every day of my life.

GENEVIEVE

(Nods) I don't doubt that.

NEAL

What you need me to do?

Taw guides Genevieve to an easy chair, then stands behind her.

Genevieve goes on studying Neal.

GENEVIEVE

(Suddenly laughs) I want you to call God up this minute and turn back the clock. I want Wayne Watkins in this room *alive*, with a signed guarantee that he'll never die.

NEAL

We all want that.

GENEVIEVE

I believe you, darling. But no, I guess you could go tell his father—though he'll be so drunk by now, he won't hear you.

NEAL

I'll call the Red Cross.

GENEVIEVE

(Waves off the idea) They've got their hands full. I doubt Wayne's the only boy died today.

TAW

I thought it had stopped.

GENEVIEVE

Never. Never does. Who was I to escape?

NEAL

A person that earned much better than this.

TAW

And will get it somehow.

GENEVIEVE

(Shakes her head No) I'm back where I started—a single woman in too big a house. The night Mother died she warned me to keep my heart in my bosom—not to rent it out to a soul that could vanish.

She loved my dad like sunrise in winter; once he died, she withered right up. Love killed her, sure as a bullet through the brain. Now it's killed me.

TAW

You'll be your old self in time—*I* know.

GENEVIEVE

You're lying, Taw. You said many times how your parents' death split you in two.

TAW

I came back together—*(Waits)* You'll be yourself far sooner than you think.

GENEVIEVE

(Nods) That's the worst news yet. Who in God's name wants to be me?

NEAL

You're a girl I've loved for thirty good years.

TAW

And me for ten.

GENEVIEVE

(Waits, then quiets them both with her hands) Eternal thanks. But one more word and I'll scream till you crack. Let's cook this supper; we can feed it to the dogs.

Taw and Neal bleakly smile at one another, then wait in place.

Genevieve stands and leads a slow procession to the kitchen.

4

Eight o'clock in the evening. The house of Roma Avery, Neal's mother. Roma is seated at the kitchen table with Porter Farwell, Neal's oldest friend and a roomer here before the war. Porter is dressed in khaki trousers and an open-necked shirt.

ROMA

So you see yourself rocking on the deep for thirty more years till you're Admiral of the Fleet?

PORTER

(Nods) It's something I can push on anyhow. I *count* somewhere for the first time ever.

ROMA

You counted here. You were my good roomer; Neal leaned hard on you.

PORTER

Many thanks. But I also see that, when I left here to risk my life on German torpedoes—well, nobody died; your path didn't swerve. It didn't exactly break my heart, but it changed my mind.

ROMA

Porter, nobody counts on the great map of things—except maybe sparrows: God watches them fall. Anybody can vanish—the world skips two steps and walks right on.

The night my father died, Mother made cheese-straws— eight dozen cheese-straws. I stirred the batter and licked the spoon. She told me then she'd depended on him for the strength to *walk*.

But she outlived his body by forty-six years and would be here now if a car hadn't hit her. *(Waits)* That doesn't mean people should just float off.

PORTER

I floated off and cherished the voyage! I don't guess I understood how much till I got Neal's letter, the single word he wrote me in three years.

By then I was docked in Liverpool after nineteen days on the winter Atlantic. He wrote one page—the local news, not a word about me. And he signed it "Till soon."

I read it on deck, facing a city grim as Hell's last basement. Then much to my shock, I tore it to shreds. I'd made Neal Avery the pole of my life, and he saw no need to say one word about me coming home or staying alive. I thought I'd weep in the presence of four more ensigns cruel as me, but I burst out laughing and knew I was *free*.

ROMA

A day hasn't passed without Neal asking if I'd heard from you. *(Laughs)* Even Taw's kept up.

PORTER

Bless her heart.

ROMA

I told her I thought she was overreaching, sending you boxes of socks and cakes.

PORTER

Socks *in* the cake—chocolate-frosted argyle socks. I'd chew them after meals, for dessert.

ROMA

Taw's come a good distance, I have to admit—and you well know I'm not her press agent. She's learned not to offer such frequent sermons; she's froze up though.

PORTER

Greeted *me* warmly.

ROMA

Then you missed the big fact.

PORTER

That she bobbed her hair?

ROMA

That she's barren as sand. *(When Porter looks baffled)* B-A-B-I-E-S. They been married nine years. But I daresay you heard no tiny thunder of infant feet down their empty hall.

PORTER

Taw's a young woman. Lots of wives postponed till the war played out.

ROMA

(Shakes her head) Lots of women Taw's age have two-headed

babies in the news every day. Last week a *six*-year-old in Bolivia bore a fat baby with fingers and toes. The priest says she got it by wading in some holy fountain.

PORTER

Got to watch those fountains—

ROMA

Throw Taw Sefton *in* one, for me!

PORTER

Taw *Avery* please.

Roma smiles and slaps her own wrist lightly, a silent "Why do I always forget?"

Neal knocks at the kitchen door.

Roma motions for Porter to answer.

He opens on Neal—no surprise (Porter's been home ten days).

PORTER

Speak of the Devil—

Neal moves in slowly.

Porter goes to the stove and pours a cup of coffee for Neal.

Neal sits by his mother and nods thanks to Porter.

ROMA

To what do I owe this personal appearance by my favorite son?

NEAL

Your first and last. I need your phone.

ROMA

Taw disconnect yours?

NEAL

I just need privacy.

ROMA

What's the hot secret?

NEAL

Wayne Watkins is dead on Okinawa.

PORTER

Since when?

NEAL

They brought me the wire, this evening at the store.

ROMA

Can't Genevieve Watkins read her own mail?

NEAL

(Waits, then slowly) They thought I'd be more merciful, Mother—I've lived in her house for nearly ten years.

ROMA

And paid good rent.

NEAL

And got a real bargain—Genevieve's kind as God.

ROMA

Kinder by far, if Wayne's really dead. Leave it to Wayne to die out of season. Did he catch the mumps or fall out of bed?

NEAL

The wire said killed. I'll call the Red Cross.

ROMA

They're in Asia, son. Who's paying for this?

NEAL

Me—your millionaire progeny.

PORTER

Let me do it. I'll know what to ask.

NEAL

(Waits) All right. But make full notes.

Porter rises and leaves through the hall door.

Roma rises and begins to clear dishes.

Neal sits in place, apparently exhausted.

ROMA

How's Genevieve now?

NEAL

Stunned. And mad.

ROMA

Is she upstairs alone?

NEAL

No, with Taw.

ROMA

Death is Taw's long suit. If she's told me once that her parents died before she could speak, she's told me a thousand tearful times.

NEAL

It made her strong. Some others broke.

ROMA

Ah? Such as who?

NEAL

(Waits) You. At age three. The night your father was shot through the heart at a white-trash teenage girl's back door.

ROMA

I raised you straight—cooked nine thousand meals and bathed your butt. I manage this house and a men's clothing store. Name one time I failed.

NEAL

(Waits) I couldn't, no ma'm. If you'd run the war, we'd have won it in a week.

ROMA

I've thought that myself. I may yet enlist in the WACs.

NEAL

(Smiles) It would change world history.

ROMA

I couldn't leave you.

NEAL

I might survive.

ROMA

Or you might die off and the Averys would perish.

NEAL

Taw's an Avery, by law.

ROMA

Taw's a childless woman; the line ends with her.

Neal has heard all this for some years now. To change the subject, he stands, moves to the refrigerator and searches its shelves.

ROMA

Hungry?

NEAL

Starved.

ROMA

There's some custard left.

Neal finds the big bowl, takes it to the table and bolts down custard with a large cooking spoon.

ROMA

Take a silver spoon—it'll seem more natural.

They both relax and laugh gently for a moment.

Then Porter returns with a note pad and joins them at the table.

ROMA

Did they know anything?

PORTER

They're still getting last-minute deaths by the hour—leftover snipers, booby traps. Wayne's commanding officer will write Genevieve. The body may well get here before then.

ROMA

A gold-star wife. Poor creature, that suits her. She lost every
race she entered; now she's won. They'll be all over the paper
this week.

NEAL

(*In quiet fury*) She's lost her world. Shame on your mouth.

*Roma rinses her hands at the sink, then moves to the table and
stands behind Neal's chair.*

ROMA

I deserved that. Thank you.

Neal does not face her but nods a grim acceptance.

*Roma looks to Porter, who gives no sign. So she quietly turns
and leaves the room.*

Neal and Porter sit in silence. Neal eats more custard.

PORTER

Watch that, buddy—it's two pounds a swallow.

NEAL

Am I gaining flesh?

PORTER

(*Looks him over*) You're better-upholstered, let us say, than in
days of yore. Of course in the Navy, you might get stuck—
everything's extra slim on board. I could prize you out.

NEAL

Couldn't prize me *in*.

PORTER

You didn't miss much.

NEAL

Just the greatest event since God said "Light!"

PORTER

It may have looked that way, from way down here. It was just long days of cheerful work with a lot of horny boys, I saw maybe three shots fired in anger, cut myself now and then while shaving, learned to walk on water. That was *my* war.

PORTER

NEAL

I'd have loved it. *(Waits)* We missed you.

PORTER

We or *you?*

NEAL

Us—you know, the whole thrilling town. Prayed for you by name every Sunday at the Holy-Roller Church.

PORTER

I trust you were there to say *Amen.*

NEAL

(Laughs) Can't say I was but I bet money on you.

PORTER

Money? Who with?

NEAL

Wayne Watkins, dead Wayne. He stayed on here months after you left, and one night he and I drove out to Palmer's Pond and downed a pint. Then Wayne stood up in the damned rowboat and flung the bottle. It hit a big rock and echoed for hours.

When the noise faded, Wayne said "Porter's dead. Neal, I know it in my *bones.*" He commenced to shiver and the boat near swamped.

To save my life, I said "Wayne, I bet you fifty dollars Porter makes it home with nothing worse than snow-white hair." Wayne said I was crazy, but at least he sat down.

Porter laughs quietly, then leans forward, takes his wallet from his trousers, searches the bills and hands Neal a fifty.

PORTER

I printed it today.

NEAL

(*Studies the bill, puzzled*) What does this mean?

PORTER

It's fifty dollars. I'm an honorable gent. Bad as Wayne's luck was, he kept me alive by betting against me.

NEAL

(*Thrusts the bill forward*) I'm solvent, Porter.

PORTER

(*Forces Neal's hand back*) Buy your first baby-boy a big silver cup from his father's best friend.

NEAL

(*Waits, then tears the bill in half and hands half to Porter*) If I have a child, I'll claim your half.

PORTER

(*Accepts his half*) Fair enough.

NEAL

But I won't come claiming, not in this world.

PORTER

You firing blanks?

NEAL

Not to my knowledge. And my parts still function.

PORTER

Something wrong with Taw?

NEAL

Not according to her. But ever since I was found unfit for service, she's pulled on back till I can barely see her.

PORTER

You asked her why?

NEAL

She always stops me by saying this is no world to bring children to.

PORTER

She meant the war surely. Give her time to relax.

NEAL

(Smiles) They teach that sort of thing in Uncle Sam's Navy—marital wisdom?

PORTER

On-board ship, boys talk about two things—food and sex. A lot of wives just clamped their knees when the first bomb burst.

NEAL

Every magazine mentions a baby boom.

PORTER

See, there's all kinds of women—

NEAL

(Smiles) And you're an expert?

PORTER

(Folds his hands prayerfully) A virgin saint.

NEAL

I was trusting you'd bloomed in the jaws of death. Those Limey girls weren't to your elegant taste?

PORTER

None I saw.

NEAL

(Studies Porter, then) Hallelujah! *(Waits)* Sex is dog business anyhow.

PORTER

(Deciding at last on candor) Not yours and mine surely?

NEAL

Ours was nothing but boys in the barn. We missed our chance.

PORTER

You thought there was a chance?

NEAL

Some days maybe, when the wind was right.

PORTER

You couldn't keep house for one short week with another
man—*(Waits)*

NEAL

I doubt I could keep house with God Above.

PORTER

I doubt He'll ask you. *(Waits)* But us—you thought there was a
chance of *what?*

NEAL

Not looking before we leaped for once—you always asking why
we took every step. You can't ask Fate for road maps, Porter.
You lunge, in the dark.

PORTER

You can't lunge for *life*, right on to the grave.

NEAL

What the hell else you think I'm doing? *(Lunges at random in
the air with his fist)*

PORTER

(Waits, then smiles) I'm forced to admit you kept your own
counsel.

NEAL

You were right about one thing—women are the world's main
magic for me. *(Smiles)* But girls were simple as naps, next to
you.

PORTER

You might have flown me some kind of signal.

NEAL

You wouldn't strike out for *Mexico*, much less the damned
moon. So I moved on.

PORTER

And now you're stalled.

NEAL

Cold in the road. *(Waits)* But not for lack of—*(Waits, then*

gently) Understand me now — not because I miss our old fools'
play.

PORTER

You sure we were fools?

NEAL

(Nods) Sick drunk—blind roaming—wrecking things and people. That doesn't mean I'm not grateful to you for—

*Porter thuds on the table with both fists, not violently but as a
final gesture. He stands, moves straight to the sink, draws a glass
of water and drinks every drop. Then he walks to the back-
porch door, pulls it open and looks outside—full dark by now.
He laughs a sudden note and continues with slightly forced
cheer.*

PORTER

I'm outward bound, on the early train.

NEAL

You've got a week left.

PORTER

I changed my mind. I plan to *leap.*

NEAL

For what I said? That's ancient history.

Porter turns back slowly and faces Neal.

PORTER

It was daily bread for me, long years. *(Waits)* No, it's what I'd
say if I stay much longer.

NEAL

Say it now.

PORTER

(Waits) No, Captain. Not *this* black night. It'd ruin us both—
me anyhow.

In the hall, the telephone rings out loudly.

NEAL

The Red Cross maybe—

Porter moves to answer but they hear Roma's muffled voice. Porter returns to stand by the table.

Neal rises in place as Roma comes to the door in her robe.

ROMA

Genevieve Watkins shot herself.

PORTER

Jesus!

NEAL

(Already moving toward the door) Porter, I need you.

Porter turns back to Roma with a calming gesture, then follows Neal out.

Roma slowly goes to the door, watches their leaving with an unseen wave, then turns and walks to the head of the table. With sudden force, she seizes the chair-back to steady herself.

ROMA

(Firm conviction) My hateful mouth. I killed that child.

Stands in place, slowly calming.

5

Eleven o'clock at night. A small waiting room in the town hospital—standard bleak furniture and old magazines. Porter slumps in a chair, leafing through a Saturday Evening Post.
Taw approaches the door and stands till he sees her.

PORTER

Any word?

TAW

(Moves to the opposite chair and sits) The bullet's still in her. If she makes it, she may never walk again.

PORTER

Was it just one bullet?

TAW

(Nods) To me it seemed like six or eight. *(Shuts her eyes, waits)* We washed all the dishes, then turned on the radio—nice soft music. I've been hooking that rug; so hot as it was, we worked on that. There wasn't much talk.

In a while though, Gen said "Will I know if it's Wayne?" I didn't understand and she said "The body—it could be anybody killed the same week as Wayne." I told her they took extra pains with that.

PORTER

(Nods) They do.

TAW

She ate a dish of peach ice cream and seemed some better. By then Neal had hugged her and gone to his mother's. Gen and I made up the daybed so she could sleep with us. She stepped back and took one long look, smiling. Then she said "Ain't it *narrow?*" And before I could try to cheer her again, she said she'd run up and get her nightgown.

I heard footsteps head into their bedroom, then a normal silence. Then a roar like nothing I'd ever heard. Mixed in with the shot was some kind of scream, like a trapped thing trying to tear off its leg.

PORTER

You ran straight to her?

TAW

(Waits, nods) No butcher shop ever looked red as that wall. She'd backed herself up in a far corner, so as not to flinch.

PORTER

Women don't use guns—mostly poison or gas.

TAW

When they want you to save them. *(Waits)* I've been in some corners myself—black holes—but never to where I couldn't see light.

PORTER

(Starts, hesitates, then decides to tell her) I actually tried it, when we finished high school.

TAW

For what? *(When Porter frowns)* I'm sorry—

PORTER

(Waits, then smiles) No, you might need it one day for your memoirs—*Great Saints I Have Known.* See, the year before we graduated, Thomas Wolfe published *Look Homeward, Angel*—the first bestseller by a native son. Everybody over six years old in the state thought they were in it, and his hometown friends got thirsty for blood.

So Neal's idea of a graduation trip was to drive to Asheville and explain to Wolfe's mother why the book was so *fine*—Neal thought even Shakespeare had seldom done better. Anyhow the mountains then were far off as Poland.

But we got there alive and trucked up the walk to Mrs. Wolfe's boarding house, a nice old place. Neal knocked and here came the actual mother of the world's greatest author. She stood about three feet tall, in heels, and had those utterly perfect false teeth, that won't let you smile. But she sat us in the parlor, and Neal commenced to sing Tom's praises.

She gave him three minutes, then raised a frail hand and said "I'll rent you boys a clean room cheap and all you can eat, but I'm too deaf to hear you. You ought to find Tom. Tom's got time to *burn*."

That was all Neal wanted—*where was Tom?* But by then I could smell her—she'd been slicing onions—and you know I'm violent around chopped onions. I burst into gigantic tears and Neal had to lead me out, mad as hell and eternally shamed. I'd ruined his chance at a lifetime friendship with the next thing to Christ on the human Earth.

TAW

(Laughs) So you shot yourself for onion tears?

PORTER

(Laughs) Tears and a little more. See, Neal planned to camp us on some exposed cliff. So with dark coming down, he drove us out toward Weaverville. In bitter silence we set up camp, built a fire, cooked beans. By then it was dark and all but freezing. My teeth chattered some but I still didn't speak.

Finally Neal said "I won't ever walk down the *road* with you, much less meet a lady." Then we both tried to sleep in thin blankets. Trouble was, we'd downed some bad corn liquor; and once Neal snored, I crawled to the car, got the shotgun and sat on the fender.

(Mimes the following) I held both barrels under my chin, said "God, forgive me" and pulled one trigger. *(Waits)* In the next split second I thought "Oh hell, I didn't mean *this*." *(Stops as if finished)*

TAW

I don't see a scar.

PORTER

(Rubs at his chin) The first trigger clicked. I stayed there, gathering nerve for the second. But Neal sat up way over by the fire and said "You can't even *die*, damn your soul." Then he laughed; I joined him and thought I'd gamble on life awhile.

TAW

Thank the Lord at least. *(Waits)* You've meant a lot to him — all the letters he wrote you.

PORTER

(Puzzled) I got precisely one letter.

TAW

(Puzzled too) He sat at the table many an evening and wrote you pages.

PORTER

Then they're at the bottom of the north Atlantic or in Neal's sock-drawer.

TAW

(Shakes her head) One more mystery.

PORTER

If you ever find them —

TAW

I won't. He's got his lockbox at the store. *(Waits)* He's locked *himself.*

PORTER

But you both seem stronger.

TAW

Porter, do we? Two or three nights a week, I wake in the dark and find Neal gone and the sheets cold beside me. I lie still and listen — he's always there, standing in the midst of the dark living room or kneeling at the ledge of the bedroom window. I drift off to sleep and, always at dawn, he's back beside me.

PORTER

What's haunting him now?

TAW

All I can find is, he's somehow shamed that the service wouldn't have him. Neal said "Flat feet are a sad damned reason to turn down a man who can shoot off a fly's knee at two hundred yards."

PORTER

Has that changed how you feel about him?

TAW

Maybe he has seemed a little pathetic. But no, no big change *I* can feel. *(Altering tack)* He's missed you a lot; he's glad you're home.

PORTER

(Shakes his head) I just signed on for life with the Navy.

TAW

Lord—that'll sadden Neal. He was counting on your help at the store, your good sense. I keep hoping it's just his age—the early thirties are a hard time for men.

PORTER

(Waits) Neal needs a son.

TAW

What makes you say that?

PORTER

(Waits) Taw, it looks like to me we ate Neal *up*—this town, you, me and Miss Roma. *(Smiles)* See, we watched Neal's face and his stylish moves and told ourselves he was bringing us *news*, from God or wherever. And maybe he did but it turned out our long worship was all he had in the world, and it wore him *out*.

Then we grew up and looked elsewhere. Neal's nothing now but a golden boy as thin as foil. All I can guess is, he needs a new target—a thing *he* can love, that won't need him.

TAW

I help him, every instant I can—

PORTER

But he can't *see* us now. He'd see his own son.

TAW

Or daughter.

PORTER

(Waits, nods) A girl might serve.

TAW

Children don't serve. Read the child-labor laws.

PORTER

I just meant, a child could stem his tide — let him send love *out*, not sit and drown in it.

TAW

He said this to you? *(Waits)* Did he say I refused?

PORTER

Yes, in a way.

TAW

God is my witness, I've begged for a child —

Neal has stood in the door through the end of that; his face conceals how much he has heard. He only shows a deep exhaustion.

Porter sees him first.

PORTER

Is Genevieve conscious?

NEAL

Groggy but talking.

TAW

Has she asked for anything?

NEAL

Asked me to stay here beside her tonight. Porter, drive Taw home please and sleep on the couch.

Porter rises to comply.

TAW

I couldn't sleep — *(When Neal shakes his head)* Can I tell her good night?

NEAL

She knows you care.

PORTER

Think she can make it?

NEAL

If she wants to. I'm working on that.

TAW

I'm her friend too.

NEAL

Taw, she made herself clear — "Neal, don't leave me please, one instant." *(To Porter)* You leaving early like you said?

PORTER

Not if you say wait.

NEAL

Wait. *(Smiles)* I'll see you when I see you.

Neal moves to Taw, kisses her once on the crown of the head, then stands her up by raising her hands.

Taw is dry-eyed but pained.

TAW

I'll stay home from school.

NEAL

Don't. I'll call you at lunch.

TAW

Or sooner.

NEAL

It's up to Gen.

Porter holds out a hand to draw Taw forward.

Taw touches Neal's face, then turns and leaves with Porter.

Neal sits in the chair that Porter left. In ten long seconds, tears flood his eyes. He does not touch his face; his hands stay flat on his parted knees. In the moments it takes to compose himself, the lighting in the room dims slightly — more to suggest the passage of time than to herald the supernatural. There is no implication that Neal falls asleep. If anything, he is unnaturally alert.

6

An instant later Genevieve appears in the doorway. She wears a floor-length white surgical gown. Through its sheer texture we see a huge blood-soaked bandage on her abdomen. That, and her uncombed hair, are the first hints of death. She has died only minutes ago in her room but has come to find Neal for candid answers to long-held questions. Her first words come from the doorsill, an almost natural voice.

GENEVIEVE

(Looks around) Fine. We're alone.

NEAL

Taw begged hard to tell you goodbye.

GENEVIEVE

Now I wish you'd let her.

NEAL

You plainly said you wanted just me.

GENEVIEVE

I must not have known I was set to die.

NEAL

(Unshocked, studies her closely) I'm not sure I'd know, except you're walking.

GENEVIEVE

And peaceful again.

NEAL

It feels that good?

GENEVIEVE

Different, to say the very least. *(Examines her hands and arms closely, hugs her shoulders slowly)* I used to could hear the blood in my ears, when the room got quiet. I used to could feel it rush through my hands. Now nothing's moving. I'm extremely still.

NEAL

(Points to a chair) Will they let you sit down?

GENEVIEVE

(Waits to know) Apparently so. *(Slowly she crosses the floor and sits, well forward, in a different chair—not the one Neal indicated. She leans to the magazines on the table, opens the top one, shuts it at once)* I can't do that. *(Faces Neal again)* How do I look?

NEAL

A touch blue round the gills. *(Waits)* Like a friend of mine named Genevieve Watkins, born Genevieve Slappy.

GENEVIEVE

Over here I've laid the *Slappy* to rest. Not that I chose to die just for that.

NEAL

(Waits) Why did you?

GENEVIEVE

(Strains to recall, then laughs) Why did I?

NEAL

Wayne got killed; we got the news. Was there some other reason?—you really loved life.

GENEVIEVE

Wayne? Killed?

NEAL

They brought me the wire; Taw read it to you.

GENEVIEVE

(Slowly recalls) Taw *told* me, blunt as a dynamite breakfast. *(Waits)* I never loved life—you had me wrong. I was scared ice-cold, every step of the way.

NEAL

You sure gave a good imitation of fun.

GENEVIEVE

(Waits to recall) It was real fun, sure—all your jokes; you were my big help. But no, I was petrified more times than not.

NEAL

By what?

GENEVIEVE

(Looks down at herself again) Being dead and alone. I watched more than one of my kinpeople die—they looked so lonesome, like children at dark. I tried to love them, but I knew they'd leave. So love and death kept me in a state. This seems some better. *(Looks around once more)*

NEAL

Know anything new?

GENEVIEVE

Who wins the World Series? *(Waits)* Sorry, not yet.

NEAL

Judgment Day—what's the schedule for that?

GENEVIEVE

Neal, show some respect. I didn't get here without big pain.

NEAL

You hurting now—any punishment?

GENEVIEVE

What on Earth would they punish me for?

NEAL

Suicide's not exactly praised in the Bible.

GENEVIEVE

(Waits) Maybe pain comes later.

NEAL

Surely they don't play tricks out there.

GENEVIEVE

(Waits) How are *you?*

NEAL

Sad to lose you. But otherwise strong.

GENEVIEVE

Don't lie to me. You're no stronger than a baby mole drug out in the sun.

NEAL

Where am I weak?

GENEVIEVE

I watched your eyes these last few years. I heard you those nights—full moon, four o'clock—humming songs to nothing but crickets and the night.

NEAL

Normal insomnia.

GENEVIEVE

Abnormal heartbreak, from what I heard.

NEAL

(Waits, nods) Heartbreak.

GENEVIEVE

Over who?

Neal stands and moves to the door, leans out to check the hall for people. Then satisfied with the privacy, he moves round the waiting room throughout what follows—upright, back to his chair, up again.

NEAL

Gen, I—do—not—know. Most souls I meet give me better than I earn—Mother, Taw, you: hell, dogs in the street. I seldom meet a discouraging word, much less a cruel deed. *(Waits)*

So any man with my smooth luck that feels unhappy is a goddamned baby that ought to be dropped from a mountain peak on his big soft head. Those newsreels from Nazi camps—starved kids piled high as this building—and here I stand in a steady moan.

GENEVIEVE

You left out Porter from your list. Porter loved you the most.

NEAL

I abused his goodness. *(When Genevieve nods)* He's found a home in the Navy at last.

GENEVIEVE

No shortage of boys to rescue there.

NEAL

Meaning what exactly?

GENEVIEVE

Meaning I've wondered were you all—peculiar: you know, queers?

NEAL

I might have loved Porter, now and again—kind skin has mostly felt good to me. *(Smiles)* But Porter seldom got past those long looks.

GENEVIEVE

He could *yearn*, couldn't he? But he'll do fine; he needs less than us. *(Waits)* What about me?

NEAL

You know I loved you.

GENEVIEVE

(Teasing) That body I had, those gorgeous curves.

NEAL

You were Wayne's, remember? I tried to be decent.

GENEVIEVE

There are no medals over here—where I am—for stingy behavior.

NEAL

Thanks. I'll keep it in mind for the future. But now, as I said, I stand here moaning.

GENEVIEVE

You stand in your life; it's all you've got. You need to be happy.
(Waits) I can tell you how—on one hard condition.

NEAL

Name it.

GENEVIEVE

Obey me. Completely. Get out of this awful room, and do what
I say.

NEAL

(Still calm but intent) I swear.

GENEVIEVE

(Firmer than ever) Swear in *blood*. Your past oaths have *not*
stood up to time.

NEAL

This one will. I hurt too much.

GENEVIEVE

(Waits) Get you a child.

NEAL

(Strains forward) Once more please.

GENEVIEVE

A human child.

NEAL

Why, in this mean world?

GENEVIEVE

You're dying at the heart.

NEAL

(Waits, then eases slightly) I can't obey you without some help.

GENEVIEVE

Learn how to get it. Taw's just scared. Losing your parents
before you can talk is no big encouragement.

NEAL

I still can't make Taw quit the past—

GENEVIEVE

Taw? Hell, you're still wearing ostrich plumes as you charge the Yankees at Jeb Stuart's side.

NEAL

Gen, you may be losing your grip. I'm as realistic as a week of migraines. I balance our books at the store every weekend; Taw and I've had nothing worse than squabbles in the past eight years; we're diligent workers, take a week at the beach —

GENEVIEVE

You're going blind fast when you need new eyes.

NEAL

I can't leave town — Taw's settled in her job; Mother can't spare me.

GENEVIEVE

Don't move two steps. I never said that.

NEAL

Sorry — talk on.

Genevieve sits a long while silent. Through these last exchanges she has started withdrawal from the visible world. It affects her voice, her sense of here and now (though any suggestion of "ghostly" stereotypes must be avoided: no high quavery voice etc.).

GENEVIEVE

About what?

NEAL

Your advice. You were telling me all I had to know.

GENEVIEVE

(Slowly) I thought I did. *(Studies his face)* What was your name?

NEAL

Neal. Still is.

GENEVIEVE

Neal. I remember. Let me say goodbye. *(Slowly she rises and starts to turn)*

NEAL

Is Wayne there yet?

GENEVIEVE

Wayne?

NEAL

Our friend.

GENEVIEVE

I seem all alone.

NEAL

Come back a min—

GENEVIEVE

To where? *(Moves toward the door)* For what? *(Faces Neal)*

NEAL

(Knows she is past reach) I loved you.

GENEVIEVE

Should I say thanks?

NEAL

Go your way. I'll work on my promise.

GENEVIEVE

What promise please? *(Waits a long moment, then turns and leaves—a gradual departure till, far upstage, only her smiling face is left as she speaks)* Thank you, hear?

Neal sits awhile. The lights rise slightly. He calmly stands and walks through the same door.

ACT TWO

1

Midnight, the small front room of the home of Dob Watkins, Wayne's father—the air and surroundings of a widower who lives alone and drinks heavily, with no woman's hand to clean behind him. A big old radio is tuned to shortwave, a stream of rapid Spanish voices—the Cuban news. Dob sits, apparently absorbed in the sound. His clothes are clean but disheveled; his white hair is unusually long for the time. A .22 rifle lies on his lap. As he hears footsteps, he aims it at the door.

Neal approaches the door and knocks once. When he hears no answer, he steps inside; then—with some difficulty—finds Dob in the darkness.

NEAL

Dob, you scared me!—thought you were a Mexican desperado. *(When he gets no answer, he points to the radio)* You understand that?

DOB

I understand you broke in at midnight. I'm drunk and poor. Who the hell are you?

NEAL

(Raises both arms in sign of surrender) Wayne's old friend, Neal Avery—remember?

DOB

(Half-lowers the gun, waits to think) If I had till sunup, I very well might. *(But slowly he props the gun by the radio and points to a chair)* I'm too short of company to kill you.

NEAL

(Takes the straight chair) Haven't had the pleasure in—what?—ten years.

DOB

(Works to think, returns to his chair) Fifteen, next month—nineteen and thirty. Dove season. You and Wayne made me take you dove hunting.

NEAL

Right—and Porter Farwell. Brought home more doves than the Law allows.

DOB

Not me. I never broke a hunting law yet.

NEAL

Wayne did. Wayne terrorized all the beasts.

DOB

You speaking of my second wife's boy—Wayne?

NEAL

Her only one, yes sir—funny, red-headed.

DOB

Never trust a red-head.

NEAL

Wayne never hurt a gnat.

DOB

Killed a world of doves. You just said so.

NEAL

(Gently edging his way toward the news) You heard from him lately—Wayne, overseas?

DOB

(Waits) I got letters here I hadn't read yet. *(Points to the shelf, a stack of mail)* Germany, Austria, Guadalcanal. Kids writing me, claiming they're all my sons. I've *had* some sons—married four times. I was that big a fool.

NEAL

(Laughs) I always wondered were you truly married. Didn't you just have arrangements with girls? Aren't all those girls still living round here—gray-headed old women?

DOB

Mean as hot rattlers. They spent me blind.

NEAL

Wayne's mother was good—used to cook us biscuits.

DOB

They all cooked biscuits. Thought biscuits for breakfast would keep me home. Took more than biscuits to hold me down in my women days. Now I can't walk fast enough to piss in the woods.

NEAL

You look well rested.

DOB

Not me. I'm worked to death by dreams. I dream bolt upright day and night. *(Points to the radio)* This Spaniard here's my main relief. *(Switches the radio off)* Say your name again.

NEAL

Neal Avery—Roma Avery's boy.

DOB

(Laughs finally) Roma—Miss *Rome.* She and me was in school, same age, together. Rome could outtalk a parrot with a college degree and patent-leather shoes.

NEAL

She wins most games.

DOB

Every damned one she plays. I saw her last Friday at the grocery store. I told her she looked good as dew on a rose. She said "Dob, thank you. This rose has got briars." *(Waits)* She outright killed your dad, understand.

NEAL

He and Mother seldom saw eye to eye.

DOB

Eye to eye! Roma dropped him like a gut-shot hog.

NEAL

(Nods) Miss Roma's been known to set a hard pace.

DOB

You're looking all right. That schoolteacher treating you good, I hope?

NEAL

Satisfactory. She's keeping *her* looks.

DOB

Can't say I've seen her lately, but she come here looking like a colt in clover.

NEAL

Now she's a high-stepping mare at least.

DOB

I always picked them ugly. Got less ambition, show you gratitude. I've lived with women would stop a damned steer in the road—that ugly.

NEAL

(Looking around) You do your own cleaning here? Cook your meals?

DOB

I don't eat. *(Laughs)* Spend all my time dusting. You pick up dust when you get to my age. *(Ruffles his hair)*

NEAL

(Waits, then a slow new tack) Wayne was in the Marines—
remember?

DOB

I think maybe so. He told me they were *men*. I told him I'd gone
to France, last war; and half the boys I met were women in
britches, specially the ones in them redcap suits.

NEAL

Wayne loved that suit. *(Waits)* He was on Okinawa.

DOB

If you say so—somewhere out yonder.

NEAL

Made it through all the fighting. Climbed Mount Suribachi,
sent us photos of it—to Genevieve. We live at her place, my wife
and I.

DOB

That Genevieve's smart, got a sock full of money.

NEAL

She was freehanded though, had a heart big as nature.

DOB

Never bought me a drop.

NEAL

(Sees an opening) Dob, she's gone.

DOB

Never asked her but once, after Wayne sailed off. She grinned
but slammed that back door fast.

NEAL

Maybe you caught her when she was down. She worried every
minute, once Wayne sailed off.

DOB

People can worry and still help their kin.

NEAL

I told you she was dead.

DOB

(Sits straight, studies Neal) Not to my knowledge, no. *(When Neal stays solemn)* Who killed her?

NEAL

She shot herself.

DOB

What got into her?

NEAL

The news about Wayne. I'm bringing you more news than I hoped to bear.

DOB

Wayne's dead.

NEAL

Yes sir—Okinawa, just recently.

DOB

(Long wait) Who have I got left?

NEAL

Clayburn for one. Spencer. Bohannon. They're all yours, I think. *(Points to the shelf)* We could read those letters.

DOB

I'll get around to it. *(Stands, goes to a corner, uncovers a Mason jar of white lightning, finds two cups, fills each and takes one over to Neal, then resumes his chair)* Who's got to pay for two big funerals? I ain't got cash to bury a squirrel.

NEAL

(Holds the cup but never drinks) The government pays for Wayne. Genevieve's got her savings.

DOB

Did they leave any will?

NEAL

Not with me.

DOB

I'm their next-of-kin then.

NEAL

Genevieve's got a brother—Dillard, in Raleigh.

DOB

Don't Wayne's insurance come straight to me though?

NEAL

I'll find out for you.

DOB

Ten thousand might just see me through—just about stake me from here to the grave.

NEAL

You're still a young man.

DOB

Young as Stone Mountain, Georgia. I was fifty-three in May.

NEAL

Then you got seventeen more years at least. God says so in scripture.

DOB

God's been wrong about me before. I pray to Jesus I don't last long.

NEAL

(Waits, then in earnest) Follow Genevieve's lead. Your gun works, don't it?

DOB

(Nods) Cleaned it last week. *(Waits)* Told you I don't break the hunting laws though.

NEAL

They couldn't arrest you.

DOB

(Stands straight to watch Neal closely) You *are* Roma's son. How did I hurt you, to get such meanness?

NEAL

You didn't. I beg your pardon; I'm tired.

DOB

I'm tired as a taxi-wheel; I hold my tongue though.

NEAL

(Nods) Still drive your cab?

DOB

Some ladies call me to haul them to church or their husband's grave. I'm the last white man from here to Raleigh with a cab-driver's license.

NEAL

You must have seen things, all those years of hacking.

DOB

I've seen my share of butts in the wind, if that's what you're after. No fun anymore—if your dick don't work, you can't watch others.

NEAL

(Shakes his head smiling) Depresses me too.

DOB

Get it caught in a door? You used to be God's gift to girls round here.

NEAL

In my better days.

DOB

What's wrong with now? More girls round here than fleas on Dave.

NEAL

Where is old Dave? Dogs smart as Dave are scarce now too.

DOB

(Points through the back wall) In the ground out there. Had to shoot him last fall; he got so blind.

NEAL

Did he ever learn all "The Star-Spangled Banner"?

DOB

No, just the first verse. Never could get him past "home of the brave." He'd break down sobbing.

They wait till silence grows heavy.

DOB

You ain't going to tell me—

NEAL

(Understands, nods) I'm as far gone as you—twenty years younger—but I've balked at the fence.

DOB

Body failed on you?

NEAL

Body works like a well-oiled rod. I've lost my will—*(When Dob shows actual interest)* will to live, just to *breathe.* I wake up every night at four A.M. My eyes click open—ten inches from Taw—and I think "Oh Christ, a whole nother day."

I lie there and I try to think "How can I make it *through?*" Then I try to guess "Through *what?*" But I can't even guess how to wait for one more dawn without yelling "*Quit!*"

DOB

(Studies Neal again) You need a preacher—a doctor at least. *I* can't help you.

NEAL

You cured old Dave. *(When Dob looks baffled)* His ears, remember—his awful mange? What was it you used?

DOB

Oh! "Happy Jack," I think they called it. Had to order off for it, two dollars a quart. Dave suffered deep torment long decades—remember?—scratching those ears. But "Happy Jack" fixed him.

(Indicates a spot on the floor) One night right here, I was rubbing him down; and oh he loved it—he'd hum sweet *hymns,* it felt so good. So I stood up, found my looking-glass and rubbed my own ears. They were cured next morning, never itched again.

(Waits) Since I shot Dave, I can't face a dog without breaking down.

NEAL

(Nods) That's me. I had my version of Dave and nothing else works.

DOB

That squatty bulldog, that you taught to dance?

NEAL

No, me—just me.

DOB

You *were* a dancer. I saw you that night you won the cakewalk.

NEAL

It was one long cakewalk—my whole life till oh maybe five years ago. Then the music failed me.

DOB

The war ruined all the good hands round here.

NEAL

I moved to the lovely music in here. *(Taps his head)* I was one great composer for a few fine years. When my body grew up and I stepped out, people smiled just to see me.

Wayne said once "Let one more girl sap your strength, and we'll have to bury you in some old matchbox—you'll be that frail." *Frail?*—every girl I loved just made me stronger.

DOB

Till you met that smart one.

NEAL

Taw? She's smart but she's been a great blessing. She curbed my drinking and running wild; but she gave me steady sweetness, which I'd never known.

DOB

Understand me now—I respect Miss Taw; but you married her, son. That'll stop all music. Angels could light on your wrist right now, singing praise in all tongues—you won't hear a note, not with that ring on.

NEAL

(Holds out his left hand, studies the ring; then stands, goes to Dob and holds out the hand) Rescue me then.

Dob grins, waits and reaches out to slip off the ring.

Neal shuts his eyes and goes still to listen.

Dob slips the ring on his own little finger.

NEAL

Not a sound. *(Waits)* You hear anything?

DOB

(Nods firmly) Just angels foxtrotting in beaded robes.

NEAL

(Opens his eyes) I'm still deaf as wax.

DOB

It's going to take time. I don't know when I last touched a woman, but it comes back to you if you wait long enough.

NEAL

You've still got kids.

DOB

One less, if you're right. No, kids don't harm you. They grow on up and your powers come back.

NEAL

Then I must need a houseful of kids.

DOB

Get your ashes hauled any night you can, but don't go claiming
Dob said "Make kids." Kids can break your heart too. You're
the damned moon and stars till they're ten or eleven. They'll
give you the time of day till they're twelve.

After that they vanish — they flat can't *see* you. They'll wait,
hand and foot, on a knocked-up strumpet they find in the road.
But you — that made them, poured food down their gullet when
their hands couldn't move — you're a filthy beat-up cheap
windbreaker they fling in the corner.

Hell, they'd give the old coat to the Salvation Army; their
dad ain't there. Or here. I'm *here*. Where in God's name are
they?

NEAL

You've got those letters.

DOB

All asking for something — birth certificates, deeds. *Deeds!* — I
don't own the stinking cot I lie on. *(Waits)* No, my heart's broke
to where it don't beat, just shivers every day or so to keep my
blood creeping.

NEAL

(Waits) But you're happy someway; even I see that.

DOB

(Surprised to believe it) Glad you noticed. I don't call it happy.
Still it's what I do. Won't change it either till the Big Boy calls
me. *(Points toward Heaven)*

*Through those exchanges, Neal has moved round the room,
touching this and that till he comes to a keg full of walking
canes. He takes out one cane, flourishes it high. Then he leans on
it heavily to walk to the door.*

DOB

Take that with you; you need the support.

NEAL

A swap for my ring?

Dob has forgot the ring on his little finger. He studies it a moment, attempts to remove it, mimes that he can't, then extends the ring to Neal.

Neal walks back, still on the cane, to accept the ring. He puts it in a pocket.

DOB

Anything I should do—with those dead children?

NEAL

I'll call Genevieve's brother in the morning. Wayne'll be on home in his own good time. I'll keep you posted.

Neal moves to the door, still using the cane but stronger now.

Dob stands in place, a farewell courtesy.

DOB

You want me to drive you?

NEAL

You helped clear my eyes. Get some rest.

DOB

Me and rest parted company a long ways back.

NEAL

(Opens the door, then points to the radio) Switch on those Spaniards then. They don't sleep either.

Dob leans to the radio, turns it on—soft popular music of the day, "Stardust."

DOB

(Moves with unexpected grace through a few dance steps) See, I told you—sweet angels in the night. They're there, if you listen. New music, all hours.

Neal conducts a bar of the music with one slow hand. Then leaning on Dob's cane, he enters the night.

Dob dances on, happy alone, a few steps. Then he turns to find Neal gone.

2

A half-hour later, Roma Avery's kitchen. Though it is one A.M., *Roma and Porter are seated at the table, drinking coffee.*

ROMA

You shouldn't have left Taw alone in that house.

PORTER

She wouldn't hear of anything less. I even offered to sit in the car in the damned driveway.

ROMA

You should have. All these sad boys coming home lately with the memory of guns—dangerous people are roaming the night.

PORTER

Call her up, Mrs. Avery. If she says Yes, then I'll go get her.

ROMA

Taw and I have a nice truce underway; one condition is I don't phone a lot.

PORTER

It'll be daylight in under five hours. No rapist could organize a raid in five hours—they got to get drunk, get their dark clothes on, their best shaving lotion. Anyhow with the war, there's barely a man in town under fifty.

ROMA

Neal's under fifty—and a good many other wrecked bodies and minds.

PORTER

Neal's no more wrecked than he's always been.

ROMA

You really talked to him?

PORTER

Long enough to tell he's the same aging boy. He just knows it now.

ROMA

Knows what exactly?

PORTER

That he used up our patience and nobody's left now to watch his act.

ROMA

His *act? (Waits)* The war sure tanned your tender hide. If Neal's life up to now was an act, then you've been the co-star, usher, projectionist, audience, janitor—

PORTER

Touché! But I seem to recall you and Taw lent a cheer—Wayne and Genevieve too. The whole town cheered; Neal was our big show.

ROMA

He did love life, strange to say—especially since he watched it so close. Most people's eyes are like fish in a cave—just not *there.* Neal saw all the world, in his own hot light, and could grin back at it. We can't turn our backs now he's stumbled on pain.

PORTER

Neal's groaned in pain since you brought him to town.

ROMA

I brought him to the *world.* He was born in this house. *(Points through the wall)*

PORTER

You put up the plaque yet—the pilgrimage site?

ROMA

(Calm force) You're a guest here, remember—a non-paying guest. Neal doesn't have to lean on the U. S. Navy for meanness and spite.

PORTER

They came with his milk.

ROMA

Beg pardon?

PORTER

(Gestures around him) These walls are soaked in spite.

ROMA

(Waits) Thank you, thank you kindly.

PORTER

You said so yourself.

ROMA

I've tried to learn better.

PORTER

(Laughs) Early this evening you gave us a fine imitation of a five-foot axe swiping off our legs—the things you said about Genevieve.

ROMA

(Nods) I did. I know. I'm profoundly sorry.

PORTER

Sorry for the millionth time just doesn't count. No wonder Neal's feelings are trapped so deep.

ROMA

Neal tells me every word he thinks.

PORTER

Then he's told you he's worse off than Genevieve and Wayne?

ROMA

When my eyes split open, each dawn, I ask myself, first thing of all, "Is Neal still here, alive on Earth? Will he come for his coffee?" See, I understand how much he hurts; and I'm scared one night he'll suddenly *go*, just die away somehow in the dark. Like my father did. Like I've meant to do, so many black nights. Help him please.

PORTER

Mrs. Avery, I had to give Neal *up*. He's Taw's and yours.

ROMA

(Searches Porter's face) You loved him better than her or me. And I thank you, every *prayer* I pray; so don't quit now, wherever you roam. Recall this truth you already know: all Taw's done is hobble Neal's legs, and I'm the worst excuse for a mother since Romulus and Remus sucked a she-wolf's tits.

PORTER

(Waits, smiles) They turned out kings of Rome after all.

ROMA

Be serious. I've ruined three lives—mine, my husband's and now my son's.

PORTER

You have been *strong*—

ROMA

Strong? Christ Jesus, I've burned every leaf; and here I sit, chewing cold dry ashes.

PORTER

(Calmly) Neal needs to hear this.

ROMA

Don't you tell him. He'll turn and go.

PORTER

Listen— *(Deliberate)* Neal Avery will see you through.

ROMA

What?

PORTER

You ready?

ROMA

Shoot.

PORTER

However much more life the cruel gods give you.

Roma sits still to take it, then turns and walks toward the outside door.

Porter rises, more than half-expecting to be shown out. Then he hears what Roma heard seconds before.

Footsteps at the outside door.

ROMA

(Whispers) Tell him and die.

Someone tries the lock.

ROMA

Friend or foe?

NEAL'S VOICE

I'm too tired to choose.

Roma stands in place.

Porter goes, turns the key and opens on Neal—no walking stick now.

Neal goes to Roma, takes her right hand.

Porter goes to the refrigerator and finds a third dish of jello.

Then he and Neal seat themselves at the table.

ROMA

Is Genevieve resting?

NEAL

Oh yes, deep rest.

PORTER

Is Dillard here yet?

NEAL

I came here to call him. *(Waits)* Where's Taw?

PORTER

She forced me to leave her.

ROMA

I'm concerned—

NEAL

Taw's all right. *(Waits)* Genevieve died. *(Waits)* An hour ago. I stopped by Dob Watkins'. He barely knew Wayne, Genevieve even less.

ROMA

Bless her poor soul. She was too young to bear it.

NEAL

(Studies Roma closely) Thank you, Mother. She's safe. Did the Red Cross call?

PORTER

I told you they might well take days.

ROMA

You can't hold Genevieve out many days.

NEAL

That's her brother's decision. Dillard's got good sense.

PORTER

(Rises) Let me call Dill. I got him through algebra and two years of Latin. *(Moves toward the hall door)*

NEAL

I don't know his number; he's a plumber in Raleigh.

Porter goes through the hall door.

Neal continues to watch Roma closely.

Roma bears the gaze. And through their exchange, they prowl the room, each doing odd jobs—smoothing a towel, washing a fork.

NEAL

Mother, I guess I'm finally grown.

ROMA

Of course you are.

NEAL

No, I never watched somebody die till tonight.

ROMA

You held your father, the moment he died.

NEAL

He wanted to go.

ROMA

So did Genevieve.

NEAL

She didn't. She'd gone upstairs for her gown. Death was just one thing that flashed through her mind, like the hymns for Wayne's funeral. The pistol waylaid her. If I'd been there, she'd be calm by now.

ROMA

You were here, son, trying to help her with plans.

NEAL

I'm always half-a-mile too far to help.

ROMA

(Firmly) You are not to blame.

NEAL

I really mean well; I'm just never *there*.

ROMA

You're where you belong—this town, your home.

NEAL

Seems like I used to have a wife—

ROMA

You do—a strong one. Go home to her now.

NEAL

I'm no good to Taw. I'd do her a favor if I plunged off in the dark
for Iceland.

ROMA

Go ask her; let her choose.

Neal goes to the central table and sits.

NEAL

(Sensing a genuine change) What's come over you? You sharp-
ened your claws on Taw for ten years.

ROMA

I stopped, just now.

NEAL

(Stares toward the ceiling) You see some light I fail to notice?

ROMA

I thought it was time to act my age.

NEAL

You learning to knit? That wouldn't become you—

ROMA

I'm serious, Neal.

Roma also sits at the table, the far end from Neal.

NEAL

Never for an instant, in all my life, have I thought you weren't
dead-down earnest.

ROMA

Son, I'm *stalled*, far worse than you. The women in my line last
forever, so what am I meant to do with all this *time* down the
road? — a lonely woman stuck up in a house with nothing to do
but run my mouth. Don't all of us need a new job? *(Waits)* Like
a child to raise?

NEAL

(Waits) Phone the orphanage; it's chocked with kids.

ROMA

Show me some honor at least—I'm old.

NEAL

(Calm but incredulous) And you need a new child?

ROMA

A grandchild that's my flesh and blood, through you.

NEAL

(Leans forward slowly) Tell me—for what?

ROMA

(Laughs) Fun. And profit. With a new chance—hell!—I could learn to live. I might have forty good years left. Don't leave me up here, mean as *I* am and bored to tears.

NEAL

I'm worse than bored; don't low-rate pain.

ROMA

I don't. But I see a world in far worse pain. The world can't end its trouble apparently. You can end yours.

NEAL

By starting a child that, in eighteen slow years, will either be a saint or a damned jailbird? *(Waits)* Genevieve stopped her troubles *quick.*

ROMA

Do it and roast in endless pain.

NEAL

You believe Gen's howling in flames tonight?

ROMA

I very much fear. She knew it when she shot; she made her choice. You're free to make yours. But remember this—if you choose to quit, her way, forever, I'll curse your soul with my last breath.

NEAL

(Smiles) You'll bless me though if I bring you a child?

ROMA

Watch me—a cornucopia of blessings! Days won't be long enough for my kind deeds.

NEAL

You understand this calls for the service of a second woman— my wedded wife? *(Covers Roma's hands with both of his)*

ROMA

Where's your wedding band?

NEAL

In my pocket.

ROMA

Why?

NEAL

Dob Watkins took it off; we played a little game.

ROMA

Not poker with Dob. You didn't lose it?

NEAL

(Reaches in his pocket, produces the ring) Good as new.

Neal studies the ring, then hands it to her.

ROMA

(Polishes the ring on her dress) Not quite. Gold wears poorly; it's softer than skin. Put it on; you'll lose it.

Roma holds it a long moment, puts it on Neal's finger.

NEAL

Till death do us part?

ROMA

(Smiles, nods) Nothing less, I hope.

NEAL

I'll work on that.

Porter's footsteps sound in the hall; he stands in the door.

ROMA

Get him?

PORTER

His wife—Dillard's fast asleep. I told her to let him rest on now; she says anyhow they'll be here by noon.

NEAL

(Rise) I'll go home and wait.

ROMA

And sleep. I've still got the pills from when your father died—knock an elephant out.

NEAL

(Shakes his head) I may need all my strength before day. *(Moves toward the outside door)*

PORTER

When will we see you?

NEAL

I eat breakfast here most days of my life.

PORTER

Want a ride home? You look fairly pale.

NEAL

Just my natural virtue, glowing at night. *(Still manages a slow broad smile)* Remember?

PORTER

(Waits) Now I do.

ROMA

Tell Taw to call me. I know all Genevieve's kin and can help.

NEAL

She'll be glad of that.

ROMA

Sleep.

NEAL

Same to you—deep rest.

Neal raises both hands beside his head, a half-conscious sign of benediction. Then he silently leaves.

ROMA

That boy may be stronger than he knows.

PORTER

I hope he knows soon.

ROMA

I told him. You tell him tomorrow morning.

PORTER

If morning gets here —

ROMA

(Rising and stretching to yawn) It frequently does. Course, I've known exceptions.

They both move to leave.

3

A quarter-hour later, Neal and Taw's living room. Two lamps burn dimly; the radio plays softly, light music of the time. The lock in the hall door turns and Neal enters. He moves carefully toward a bowl of fruit, newly set on the table. He studies it a long while, plainly exhausted. Then he takes an apple and bites into it audibly.

At the sound, Taw silently opens the bedroom door and stands. She wears a floor-length housecoat but is otherwise neat, her hair in place.

Neal has not heard or seen her.

TAW

I didn't expect you.

NEAL

(Not facing her) I didn't expect one thing that happened this whole long day. *(Turns to see her)* Sorry I woke you.

TAW

I was awake, just waiting in the dark.

NEAL

(Gently) I asked you not to stay here alone.

TAW

I couldn't bear the thought of that room up there. *(Points overhead)* I came back and scrubbed it all down, hard.

NEAL

I'm sorry you had to be the one. *(Waits)* Dillard and his wife'll be here by noon.

TAW

Much as Dill loved her, I thought he'd rush. *(Waits, then understands)* She's dead—Genevieve.

NEAL

(Nods) There's no rush now.

Neal sets his apple back on the table, moves to the farthest chair and sits. Then he cups his face in his hands a long moment.

NEAL

She came through surgery fine, then—how did you know?

TAW

My dream—I must have dozed after all *(Points to the back of the house)* Gen was here—*scratching* at her own door.

NEAL

It's not hers now. *(Waits)* You let her in? —in the dream, I mean.

TAW

That must have been when you drove up.

NEAL

I left her two minutes, to see you and Porter, and she slipped off. Got her way after all.

TAW

Maybe she felt it coming on and spared you the sight.

NEAL

(Nods) Sounds like her at least.

TAW

You'd borne too much—

NEAL

(Faces her squarely) Not a feeble thing, same as ever. You faced all the blood; it's under your nails. I was no more than a sympathy card, that helpless and clean.

TAW

She asked for you. She could have said Wayne or me or Porter. But the instant I reached her, she said "Get Neal."

NEAL

I'd just known her longer.

TAW

Gen was smart; give her credit. She wanted a friend that wouldn't condemn her.

NEAL

I hope that's true; I'm no hanging judge. *(Waits)* Did she say any more?

TAW

She laughed. Said "Wouldn't my mother be proud? I put on clean underwear after lunch. Mama always said 'Be ready for Judgment.'"

NEAL

What else?

TAW

Squeezed my hand when they rolled her out but no other word. She talk to you?

NEAL

Asked me to stay there with her, like I said.

TAW

No mention of Wayne?

NEAL

(Shakes his head) She said "Taw Avery is a lonely soul."

TAW

I'm not, to my knowledge.

NEAL

(Nods) Her absolute last words, to me anyhow.

TAW

(Calm but in deep concern) Gen got that wrong.

NEAL

Gen could smell unhappiness through concrete.

TAW

(Firmly) She got me wrong.

NEAL

(Waits) Mother agrees with her. Porter too—I think they blame me.

TAW

(Strokes her cheeks) I washed my face two hours ago and *thought* I knew it.

NEAL

They claim you and I are stuck in the shoals.

TAW

It's *our* life—I'll tell them tomorrow. We're fine. *(Waits)* The shoals of what?

NEAL

Self-pity, middle age.

TAW

We're barely weaned. I move strong as ever; I like my work; you and I lope along here very well; your mother and I—

NEAL

I'd like to believe you but tonight I don't. We been married nine years; we're dead in the road.

TAW

(Still calm but gaining force) Where were we going please? — I'm *settled,* here. I spent my childhood trekking this state, hoping to find one spot I could light. But nobody honestly wants an orphan — we're too damned scary.

You made me this home and proved you *meant* to. We're living the life I craved so hard my knuckles bruised every time I prayed — I begged that hard. If I get fifty more years like this, I'll need eternity to pay my thanks.

NEAL

I hope you get it — eternity.

TAW

With you, Neal Avery. Otherwise, I pass.

NEAL

I doubt they let you choose.

Neal studies her closely, shaking his head. What follows is all intense but muted by sadness and exhaustion.

TAW

You don't want to see us with harps and gold curls?

NEAL

It's not what I want; it's what *we* need. Maybe we ought to live like the humans, the rest of the poor old human race. *(When Taw looks baffled)* I think we may very well need something as plain as children, one child at least.

TAW

(Waits, smiles) Children aren't meant to solve problems. And prospective parents ought to get licensed by an expert board —

NEAL

Composed of you and how few others?

TAW

I'm serious; this is adult business. Anyhow I teach till June.

NEAL

(Counts on his fingers) If we start now, he'll come in June.

TAW

(Faces Neal intently and waits) He? Your magic powers return-
ing? *(Then also counts on her fingers and smiles)* I'd look like a
battleship, the last months of school.

NEAL

The kids could draw big pictures of you—Mount Taw at sunset. Seriously, sweetheart—Gen, Mother and Porter all
brought it up, and on their own.

TAW

One more time: it's—none—of—their—goddamned—business.

NEAL

In one way, it is—we ask for their help; and lately they've
started trying to give it, but here we sit perfecting our woes.

TAW

I—am—*not*—woeful.

NEAL

Sure, you're ticking like a well-made clock; but you long since
gave up knowing the time. *(When Taw's face objects)* You *don't;*
I don't. Every trace of our sweet old, safe old world is dead as
this floor. We think we've put a lid on something called World
War Two. We're idiots!

The bodies that stump back here from this last war will turn
this place, this town and country, to the *moon* by Christmas.
Christ, we'll need a whole new language, to order beef stew at
the Downtown Cafe.

You'll meet every challenge, I have no fear. You'll teach moon
grammar by New Year's Day. But me?—Neal Avery's as near
an antique as that oak hatrack in Mother's back hall and a lot
less useful.

(When Taw has no answer) My brief career as social chair-man of a crossroads town is long since over. I need a grown human life to live, some job to do outside my head and be some *use* to the pitiful Earth.

Till I get it, I'm poisoning you. Poison's rising, as we wait here. I know it's up to *my* lips now.

TAW

You're grieving for Gen —

NEAL

I'll grieve for Gen long as I draw breath — but Taw, I'm finally so bone-tired I can't keep telling easy lies. You and I, and the air around us, are frozen *still.*

TAW

(A last self-defense) Neal, my darling, we're both past thirty. So maybe we don't have a lot yet to show — on paper, in the sky. But we're walking the path most humans walk.

We've hurt a minimum of people and dogs; we meet each other with courtesy, most days. Neither one of us planned a lot more —

NEAL

(Smiles) That's a shameless set of lies.

TAW

It's the truth *I* know.

NEAL

You never complained, outside this room?

TAW

Never. *(Waits)* I talked to Genevieve —

NEAL

(With growing depth) That's a black lie. You think I'm cracked. You've made that plain to my family and friends, and you want a way out.

TAW

(Impressed but calm) Stop. Be fair. This is what I'd tell God, if

He strode in I don't feel fooled or cheated or trapped. You're the same strange boy I married and loved. *(Waits)*

But Lord, two of our friends *died* today. We're sad and ragged. We need to stop thinking and lie down to sleep.

NEAL

Sleep is as likely as Wayne walking in with souvenirs—fresh coconuts, dud hand grenades. *(Almost unconsciously half-extends his arms toward Taw)*

TAW

(Stands in place) Things far stranger have happened on Earth.

NEAL

Such as?

TAW

Spring coming each year, Christ rising from the tomb. But no, for strangeness you may very well be stuck with me—the girl that chose you, your personal savior.

NEAL

Don't be sacrilegious.

Past the height of their quarrel, they are still more exhausted. From here to the end, they talk and move with the slow and sober grace of creatures rendered nearly transparent by baffled grief.

TAW

I'm not. *(Strokes her own arms)* I'm solid human flesh. That's sacred as anything in this world.

NEAL

I don't doubt you.

TAW

Can you feel it from there?

NEAL

Al-most. *(Waits)* You said we were tired.

TAW

I was, when I said it.

Neal suddenly shivers hard.

TAW

You catching cold?

NEAL

I thought I saw Gen. *(Rubs his eyes)*

TAW

We got to believe sweet Gen's at peace.

NEAL

(Nods) I must be groggy. What woke you up?

TAW

(Waits, then slowly) The pure sight of you.

NEAL

(Still hungover from his shaky moment) I may be a ghost. Maybe I died too. Maybe I drove out toward the river, once Gen was gone, and plugged my brain with a cold lead shot.

TAW

From here you look like the boy I chose.

NEAL

The ancient child. But see, you can poke right through my skin—I'm ec-to-plasm. *(Raises a hand, spreads the fingers, then pokes between them with the other hand)* I'll evaporate any instant now.

TAW

Then we're wasting time.

NEAL

(Stands, his face clearing) You believe in ghosts?

TAW

I hope not. Lord, name one thing worse than nosing round your aging friends—

NEAL

For this ghost here to love flesh fine as yours and not touch it.

TAW

(A short but real shudder) That might be arranged.

NEAL

Who by?

TAW

Taw S. Avery, 212 Beech Street.

Neal moves toward her—one hand out before him, unsure as the blind.

Taw moves to meet him and takes the hand.

TAW

Feels real to me.

NEAL

You do, to me. *(Kisses her neck)* I seem to recall this might be a time.

TAW

When what?

NEAL

When we might start something new.

TAW

(Rests her head on his chest) It might well be; I'm getting no younger.

NEAL

Very few humans are.

TAW

(In earnest) Or ghosts.

NEAL

I'm the ghost; that's my line please.

TAW

Very few ghosts talk.

NEAL

(Clamps his lips down hard, makes low dumb noises—more
eerie than comic) Mm, mm, mmm.

Taw draws back from him, turns, moves toward the bedroom.
Hand on the door, she turns back unsmiling.

None of this is young-married coy to either of them. It has the
taste of a thoroughly serious recognition of new self-knowledge,
this side of despair—tonight or never, some bold change must
start.

TAW

I'm shutting our door behind me now. Ghosts can walk
through doors—

She opens the door, walks through slowly and shuts it quietly.

Neal waits, then rises, walks to the table—the remains of his
apple. He lifts it and takes one more loud bite. Then he loosens
his tie, switches off the radio, turns and follows Taw.

4

Immediately after, Taw and Neal's empty living room. A long
moment after Neal leaves for the bedroom, the lights alter
silently—dimmer, then gold.

   The hall door opens and a man walks in silently, door ajar
behind him. It is Wayne Watkins, still dressed in the clean-
pressed Marine uniform in which he was killed on Okinawa. No
blood, no dirt and his clipped hair is neat. He seems mildly
puzzled by the new surroundings; he moves to the midst of the
room and turns all ways to see it. He moves to the bedroom door
and leans to listen. If he hears any sound, he makes no response.
He stands still a moment, moves to the table, raises Neal's apple,
sniffs at it carefully, sets it down. Then he takes an unbitten

apple from the bowl and rubs it clean on the flank of his trousers.

Unnoticed by Wayne, Genevieve stands in the open hall door. She wears a clean crisp version of the dress in which she shot herself. Her hair is immaculate. She does not see Wayne but walks through the room to the radio and switches it on—soft music that gradually rises to the threshold of sound: a song of the 1930s, when they met. She rocks in place, a solitary dance.

Wayne bites his apple.

The sound reaches Genevieve; her arms fall slowly and she turns to see him.

Through the start of the scene, they are reenacting their actual meeting years ago, in adolescence. But there must be no hint of childishness or country stereotype in their speech.

GENEVIEVE

Do I know you?

WAYNE

(Turns calmly, studies her, smiles) You know my oldest brother, Bohannon.

GENEVIEVE

You favor Bo, sure. Same good eyes.

Wayne bats his eyes comically, moves a step toward her.

GENEVIEVE

(Stops him with a firm hand in the air) Wait on there awhile. You Watkins boys are known to be fast. *(But in another moment she steps a little toward him)* Most girls notice hands and wrists. Genevieve Slappy goes straight for the eyes.

If they're deep-set and brown, I run like a fox. *Blue* though and set a little too far apart—like yours are now—I hold my ground. Then if they're not frisking round the damned room, hunting somebody better, I guess it's a creature I want to know.

WAYNE

Say you're Genevieve Slappy?

GENEVIEVE

(Nods) Ain't it awful though?

WAYNE

(Freezes, eyes on her; not blinking once) I pass your test, don't I?

GENEVIEVE

Son, the Slappys are not that easy.

WAYNE

Watkinses are—we're Dob Watkins' boys. He's *taught* us stuff.

GENEVIEVE

Such as?

WAYNE

Manners. How to make girls think they dozed off in Hell and woke up, gazing at *Gabriel.*

GENEVIEVE

Who's this Gabriel?

WAYNE

In the Bible, some prince.

GENEVIEVE

(Waits) That Gabriel's the famous angel, fool.

WAYNE

You a big churchgoer?

GENEVIEVE

Ten unblemished years of Sunday school; then I quit.

WAYNE

But you still got, like, morals and all?

GENEVIEVE

Get that straight now! I may not darken a church door again; but believe me, I know what's right from wrong.

WAYNE

You mentioned my brother—how you know him?

GENEVIEVE

You mentioned Bo; I said "Yes I know him." As far as *how* goes, just understand—I don't stay home memorizing the Bible. I've *been* somewhere. Went to Raleigh last Sunday.

WAYNE

Did Bohannon take you?

GENEVIEVE

You studying private detection, are you? A lifetime peeping through people's keyholes?

WAYNE

I love my family. I was just wondering.

GENEVIEVE

Wonder's good for your hair; makes it shine and wave. I walk around, wondering, several hours a day. *(Begins her slow way around the room—touching objects, dusting things with the side of her gown)* You a natural redhead?

WAYNE

No, I dye it twice a week.

GENEVIEVE

Can't buy that color. I wish you could.

WAYNE

Most people scared of redheads.

GENEVIEVE

Most people need straitjackets too and armed guards. I think natural red hair is very distinguished.

WAYNE

Dad's snow white-headed; Ma's auburn-haired. Dad says not but one other redhead in town and he's half-colored.

GENEVIEVE

Relax. Sit back and enjoy your gifts.

Wayne obeys and sits on the sofa.

GENEVIEVE

Hold it—this is my house.

WAYNE

You said "Sit back."

GENEVIEVE

Wayne! *(Waits)* Don't mix me up! *(Again her face clouds over, confused; then she studies him)* Wayne? Wayne *Watkins?*

WAYNE

You're not having some kind of spell here, are you?

GENEVIEVE

No, I'm all right. *(Moves to a chair and sits compactly)* You don't have any smelling salts, I bet.

WAYNE

Had some liquor but my two buddies drunk it.

GENEVIEVE

Neal Avery was one, I bet my last dime.

WAYNE

And Porter Farwell—he throws up early though.

GENEVIEVE

(Studies his face again, still incredulous) Wayne? I—

WAYNE

(Now genuinely baffled) Yes ma'm?

GENEVIEVE

Stop calling me *ma'm;* you're two years older—*(A long wait)* They said you were dead.

WAYNE

Who in hell?—

GENEVIEVE

(Nods) Your fine friend Neal, his wife—who?—Taw. Said you got shot by a sniper—when was it?

WAYNE

(Waits) I did. I forgot. *I'm* sorry. *(Looks round)* What am I doing here?

GENEVIEVE

To see me, I hope.

WAYNE

Genevieve Slappy?

GENEVIEVE

—That *was*. I took your name eight years ago.

WAYNE

Welcome to it. But please, ma'm—why?

GENEVIEVE

I loved you that much.

WAYNE

I appreciate it, lady, but—

GENEVIEVE

What?

WAYNE

Who—really—are—you?

GENEVIEVE

Nobody but your wife.

WAYNE

(Shakes his head, laughs) I thought getting killed was enough for one week; now I'm married too!

GENEVIEVE

You have been for years, August 1937.

WAYNE

That your wedding dress? It's *original.*

GENEVIEVE

(Studies her dress) I guess it must be what I was wearing when I went to the clinic.

WAYNE

You sick or something?

GENEVIEVE

In the same boat as you.

WAYNE

Who shot you?

GENEVIEVE

Me.

WAYNE

With my old pistol? I didn't think that thing would hit a stalled truck.

GENEVIEVE

Hit *me* broadside.

WAYNE

I'm sorry.

GENEVIEVE

How's the rest of your family? No, really—I loved you.

WAYNE

How could anybody love a Watkins that much? *(Laughs again, shakes his head; Genevieve hushes him with a finger)* Course I am a Marine. Join the Navy, see the world. Join the Jy-rines, go to Hell!

GENEVIEVE

(Looks around) This look like Hell? Looks more like the downstairs of our old house. I always liked it down here better than up, but I got better rent on the downstairs half, so I settled for heights.

WAYNE

We could repossess it.

GENEVIEVE

They treat it real well.

WAYNE

Neal and Taw?

GENEVIEVE

Now you're coming to.

Wayne sits a moment, then rises slowly and goes to Genevieve, extends his hand.

GENEVIEVE

That's a stupendous welcome! I wait here three years, worried blind, send you six letters a week, bake brownies—and now you want to shake *hands?*

WAYNE

I want to go home. I'm tired as a coon that's outrun his hounds.

GENEVIEVE

Look more like a hound, a good coon *dog.*

WAYNE

Make fine house pets, loyal and kind, eat precious little.

GENEVIEVE

They're magnets to fleas.

WAYNE

Hush.

GENEVIEVE

Hush yourself.

WAYNE

All right.

Wayne bends to the crown of her head—a long kiss. Then he steps well back and offers both hands.

Genevieve rises and enters his arms.

They hold on closely, in place a long moment. Behind them the radio music swells, a rhapsodic wordless tune of the day— "Deep Purple."

Wayne wraps an arm around Genevieve's waist and dances slowly toward the hall door. By now they have gained a whole new grace, unseen in their earthly bodies.

Genevieve pulls back, halfway gone.

GENEVIEVE

That music's bound to wake them up. *(Points to the Averys'
bedroom door)*

WAYNE

Who's them?

GENEVIEVE

(Points again) You know—

WAYNE

(Waits) I don't, no more, if I ever did. *(Takes Genevieve's chin in
hand, searches her eyes)* And you don't either.

GENEVIEVE

(Looks to the bedroom door again) Still, that music—

WAYNE

Would you just hush? They're dead to the world.

*Genevieve thinks, looks again round her former place, then
finds Wayne's eyes and gravely nods. Slowly she leans her head
to his shoulder and together they leave.*

The door shuts behind them.

"Deep Purple" pours from the radio.

BETTER DAYS

July 1974

ACT ONE

1

Noon, the kitchen of Roma Avery's house. After so many years, the room still shows traces of its nineteenth-century origins, in the moldings and door frames. Even the occasional appliance is ancient, though well kept. In a corner, a large electric fan is idle.

The door to the backyard opens and Taw Avery enters. She is dressed entirely in funeral black—gloves, small hat, purse. She walks to the table in the center of the room, slowly removes the gloves and hat, cools her face with her hand, then notices the fan. She plugs it in and stands back to bathe in its soothing wind.

The door opens again and Neal Avery enters—a dark blue suit, a dark red tie. He sees Taw cooling but goes to the table and slowly sits.

In a moment Taw turns and studies him.

TAW

Just one more minute, I'll haul out the food.

Neal nods, not turning.

Taw shuts her eyes for a few last seconds. Then she takes an apron from a hook on the wall, ties it over her dress, opens the

*refrigerator, draws out a platter of fried chicken and brings it to
the table.*

Neal faces her, puts up a hand to stop her.

NEAL

I couldn't eat a bite.

Taw stands in place.

TAW

Me either. But Cody and Porter might be hungry.

NEAL

They headed right on back out to the grave. Cody's concerned
that they cover her right.

TAW

(Shakes her head) It's hot as the hinges of Hell out there.

*Taw turns aside to a counter, sets the platter down, covers it
with a clean dishtowel. Then she moves up behind Neal and
lays her hands on his tired shoulders.*

*Neal sits still a moment, then shuts his eyes and leans back
against her.*

TAW

Neal, go in the front room and rest on the sofa; it's cooler there.

NEAL

(Taking her hands) I'll air-condition this whole house now; and
that's a promise, Taw.

TAW

Rest first. You haven't shut an eye in—what?—eight days.

NEAL

Nine. You either. Rest is for children.

TAW

You're *my* oldest child.

NEAL

(Nods) I can wait. (Releases her hands and looks around slowly)
You think it's possible?

TAW

What?

NEAL

Air-conditioning a house this old.

*Taw steps to a chair and sits at the table. She also looks around,
then smooths her hair.*

TAW

These walls are thick as a granite fort.

NEAL

Dillard Slappy just fitted out Genevieve's house, and it's cool as
Greenland. Said that was his only hope of a sale — a house that
old, all musty and damp.

TAW

(Waits) Not us here. We can't stay here.

NEAL

(Genuinely puzzled) Where else would we go?

TAW

We moved in here to help your mother and thought it would
just be weeks or months. I was glad to help, but it's been three
years.

NEAL

It's all ours now.

TAW

(Calmly) Never. It's Roma Avery's forever. We're leaving this
house.

NEAL

For where?

TAW

Madagascar. (Waits) I told you, the night we decided to come here, I'd help you see your mother to her grave—not a step beyond. Now we need our own place.

NEAL

For what?

TAW

Lord! *Life* again—we could live thirty years, just breathing again.

NEAL

(Waits) You're serious.

Taw smiles, then stands and removes the apron. The following exchange proceeds with the compressed calm of two fervent voices avoiding anger through affection, fatigue and the force of the heat.

NEAL

(Quietly) But not this minute. Jesus, have a heart.

TAW

I really don't think my heart's in question. It's ticked right on through a good deal of hell.

NEAL

So you tell me now, with her bones barely cool?

TAW

Neal, your mother's bones were cold at our wedding.

NEAL

The fact that you never knew your mother doesn't give you the right to spit on mine.

TAW

It's not spit, truly. It's a deep old hurt. *(Rubs hard at the center of her chest)* Your mother did all she could to kill me.

NEAL

(Waits, nods) You're free to go. But I live here.

TAW

I didn't say a word about leaving you.

NEAL

All you said amounts to that.

Neal stands in place. He makes no threatening move or gesture, but his whole demeanor speaks a firm rejection.

TAW

I've gone too far, too soon, I guess.

NEAL

You're goddamned right you—

A loud knock from the backyard door.

Taw looks to Neal.

Neal goes to the door and opens it.

Dob Watkins, neatly dressed, stands looking down.

NEAL

Dob. *(Waits, no answer from Dob)* Step in out of that broiling sun.

Neal steps aside and the old man enters, stops just inside.

TAW

Mr. Watkins, you're out in dangerous weather.

DOB

I am, yes ma'm. I come to your funeral.

Taw looks to Neal in bafflement.

NEAL

We buried her just a few minutes ago—the *new* cemetery.

DOB

Not out by your dad? *(Waits)* I ought to have known she wouldn't pick him to lie by for good.

NEAL

(Smiles) She picked her own plot—space for one grave.

DOB

I ought to have known. I walked two miles.

TAW

Then let me get you a glass of tea.

Neal motions Dob to a chair at the table.

Taw goes to the refrigerator for tea.

Dob carefully sits, both hands spread on the table before him.

Neal takes the glass from Taw and serves Dob, then sits beside him.

Dob sugars the tea heavily, stirs it slowly.

Taw works at the sink, rinsing earlier dishes.

NEAL

You must have known Mother long as anybody left.

DOB

All her life. She and me had us a baseball team.

NEAL

She never told me that.

DOB

A lot she never told you; Roma was a rounder.

NEAL

I bet she played backstop or umpire.

DOB

(Laughs) That was her line! No, she pitched and we seldom lost a game.

Leaving the tall spoon in his glass, Dob takes a long swallow.

NEAL

This last inning was all she ever lost.

DOB

Her heart give out?

NEAL

Amounted to that. She'd been blind, you know, the past three years. The cataract operations failed; her eyes got infected. She hated most minutes she breathed after that.

DOB

Roma was a looker, those great wide eyes. *(Waits)* Fine to look *at* too.

NEAL

She always said she was ugly as a mud fence daubed in misery.

DOB

(Shakes his head) She wasn't, not then. I thought she was sent my way by God, and I evermore wanted to court her *close*. My dad said Rome was too good for me, but she'd been kind to me at school, so finally I slicked my hair down and made my try.

I come around here — to this very same door, sixty-six years back, me just barely shaving — and I brought Rome a rouge box I'd won on a punchboard. I prayed anybody but her would come; I'd shove my box in and run for dear life.

But here come Roma in a white swiss dress, bright as daybreak on a new tin roof. I said "I won this and want you to have it." She studied and said "What would I owe *you*?" I wanted to say "All the sweetness you got," but I said what came, and it turned out truer. I said "You already paid me, Rome."

I just meant her kindness — she was sweet in school, helped me pass three grades. So her hand came out and took my box. Her face lit up and she said "Dob Watkins, I'll help you for life."

Then she shut the damned door. But I wasn't mad. She'd give me all I could hope to get — from uptown here, a house this fine.

NEAL

Was it dark wood, with a gold rose on it?

DOB

(Nods) I doubt it was *gold* —

NEAL

It's upstairs on her dresser now. She used it till a week ago.

DOB

I'm glad to know she remembered me.

NEAL

Remembered every word she'd heard, every finger she'd seen rise or fall in the air. This last year she could barely swallow, but she'd lie there while I ate beside her and tell me the menu — down to the pickles — of meals her mother packed for her brother when he went to Cuba with Teddy Roosevelt.

Taw has paused to hear that. She dries her hands and moves toward the hall door.

Dob rises quickly in place.

TAW

Please sit. I just need to change out of these hot things.

DOB

(Still standing) You make strong tea; not many women can.

Taw laughs, motions Dob down again, then leaves. She silently goes to her and Neal's bedroom, starts a small fan, removes her funeral clothes, then lies to rest in her slip.

NEAL

Sit down. I'm glad of your company.

DOB

(Begins to sit) You miss her already?

NEAL

These last three years, I prayed many times the Lord would just take her. But Dob, she died like a gut-shot dog. She clawed at the air for every breath through eight long days.

DOB

You did right by her. I'm flat-damned lonesome as a horse in Detroit. Five or six children and nobody's ever said "Come live here."

NEAL

You still in your house?

DOB

My piece of a house—you come there the night they killed Wayne.

NEAL

Stay where you are. I wish my life was free as yours.

DOB

You got you a smart wife, a good paycheck.

NEAL

(Points to the door) You walked in here five minutes ago and stopped what was all but a razor fight. *(When Dob continues watching)* I step in the house from Mother's funeral, and Taw hits me full-face by saying she's *moving.*

DOB

She's too young to *stand.*

NEAL

She's not but one year younger than me, and she hates this house.

DOB

I'm eighty-two; I still like to move.

NEAL

(Looking around) Built to last till doomsday. *(An impulse— fumbles in his pocket and holds out a key)* You want it? Dob, take it.

Dob smiles but shakes his head.

DOB

Get you a new place; give this one to your boy.

Neal pulls back, stands and goes to the sink. He rinses his face in a stream of cold water.

In that brief pause, Dob's head nods forward—a quick little nap.

NEAL

You pass Cody out there?

DOB

Cody who?

NEAL

My boy.

DOB

Last I heard, he was in Vietnam.

NEAL

He was—a Marine, like your poor Wayne. Cody's lived through it though and got in last night, "compassionate leave." He and Porter are still at the grave, seeing to the flowers.

DOB

Roma couldn't stand flowers.

NEAL

(Smiles) Hated the sight. How did you know?

DOB

The Methodist Church used to have Children's Day every spring that came. We'd all have to say a verse or sing a damned hymn. The year I recall, Roma learned a poem called "The Rebel Bride"—took the best part of a day to recite; or so it felt, even looking at her.

But she finished, perfect, in a bottle-green dress. Our teacher shot forward and stuck out a rose, a big damned rose with briars long as legs. We boys were still clapping, but Rome spoke out—"Thanks to you but I won't touch a rose."

NEAL

(Still smiling) I spent the last three years, fending off flowers.

She'd tell me "Neal, I'll take them when *dead,* not one minute sooner."

                    DOB

She's liable to rise up now tonight and fling those wreaths halfway to Raleigh.

The sound at the yard door of feet approaching. Porter enters first in a Naval captain's uniform.

Cody soon follows in Marine dress-uniform.

Dob stands again.

                    PORTER

Dob! *(As he moves to shake hands)* It's Porter Farwell. I thought you were in Heaven too.

                    DOB

Not to my knowledge *yet,* Commander.

                    PORTER

Captain—I'm ready to retire; don't demote me.

                    DOB

Beg your pardon. *(Points to Porter's hat)* Whatever they call you, that's a big spread of gold. You bound to seen *trouble* to earn all that.

                    PORTER

(Smiles) Dodged a few torpedoes, thirty years back. The rest is just a reward for time—I gave them my life.

                    DOB

No such thing. You're a growing boy.

                    PORTER

Wrong, friend, but I almost feel it.

Porter hangs his jacket and hat on a wall hook and moves to the refrigerator.

Cody stays near the door.

CODY

Where's Mother?

NEAL

Say hey to Dob Watkins, son.

CODY

Morning, Mr. Watkins.

NEAL

Dob walked the wrong way—to the old cemetery. But he knew your grandmother longer than us. *Sit* down, Dob.

DOB

I better be shuffling.

CODY

(Steps a little forward but keeps a shield of distance well-round himself) Grandmother talked about you more and more. By the time I left, she'd replayed all your old ball-games for me.

DOB

(Still standing) Thank you, son. Old Rome and me, we *had* our day. *(To Neal)* I need to go.

NEAL

Sounds like you got a date.

DOB

A spry old widow. I mow her grass.

NEAL

(Laughs) I bet you do—*grass* indeed and a good deal else. Dob, you ain't quit yet?

DOB

I'm harmless, Neal. But I sing to her, sweet; and she cooks me a dinner.

CODY

Let me get out of this stiff suit and I'll drive you.

DOB

I won't refuse that. Can't see to drive myself. Hit a cow last

April back in the country. Farmer ran out and cut her throat right in the *road*, to bleed her fast—wouldn't let me pay him, even sent me some beef.

CODY

Just a minute.

As Cody leaves through the hall door, Porter has finished assembling his lunch. He brings it to the table and sits.

Cody climbs to his bedroom, removes his uniform and changes into cool street clothes.

PORTER

Better eat something, Dob. That widow wants strength.

DOB

She ain't complained yet. *(Slowly sits)*

PORTER

And it's extra hot out. Thirty years at sea, I'm used to the cool.

DOB

Is it truly that long?

PORTER

Thirty-two years exactly and a few odd minutes.

DOB

Seems like a week.

PORTER

It did to me, the first twenty-five years. But the Navy now is a sad proposition. Vietnam ruined *it* too.

DOB

It has been a piss-poor excuse for a war.

PORTER

Don't say it to Cody; he loves his part.

NEAL

(Uncertain) Cody tell you that?

PORTER

It didn't take words. His face looks like he's been in a game—a game he's won but with no survivors.

NEAL

He's sure-God aged ten years in one.

DOB

What is he—near forty?

NEAL

Twenty-eight years old.

DOB

He's a fine-looking fellow, but he does look *impressed.*

NEAL

He's seen some hell.

DOB

I saw it in France, fifty-seven years back—knee-deep in literal human shit and swarming with cooties. Tore up every good place in my mind. They ought to just shot me on Armistice Day. What they sent back here won't me—nobody *I* respected.

NEAL

You got some good kids.

DOB

I warned you about kids thirty years back.

NEAL

Cody's brought me rewards I didn't know existed.

DOB

He ain't dead yet. *(Sees Neal's shock)* I meant to say all his tale ain't told.

NEAL

We won't live to hear it.

DOB

I sure won't.

PORTER

You both well may. Cody's asked to go back out to our little war—forty-odd thousand dead black and white boys, a lot more yellow.

DOB

(Nods) It's been a nigger war.

NEAL

It *is* one fracas I'm glad I missed.

PORTER

You'd have loved it, boy—nobody can win.

NEAL

Beg pardon?

PORTER

Your craving for hopeless causes. This war hasn't meant but one hard thing—our Uncle Sam can lose a war: and a war any self-respecting scout troop could win in a weekend.

NEAL

We rebs lost our world a century ago.

PORTER

You rebs, not I. And not quite the world—just a few hundred lovely homes, some silver and glass, the deeds to a million or so strong blacks.

NEAL

Nearly *two* hundred *thousand* stone-dead rebel boys—

DOB

My pa lost a leg, seventeen years old. Right till he died, he'd ask me to scratch it; and it'd been lost since Second Bull Run.

NEAL

Used to give me a nickel, sometime downtown, to tie his one shoe.

DOB

Had his last child at sixty-seven—Arlene, you know her.

PORTER

Arlene—that stutters?

DOB

A spider bit her in the damned baby cradle. Can't say her own name. She can eat dinner though.

NEAL

Must weigh three hundred.

DOB

Don't tell me please; I got to eat tonight.

PORTER

Neal liked her right well in school—

NEAL

She *was* the first waterbed, long before hippies.

DOB

(Smiles) Look out, boys. She's *my* half-sister. *(Waits)* We all enjoyed her, sweet Arlene. She's pitiful now.

NEAL

So's everybody here.

PORTER

I've seldom felt better.

NEAL

Your life's all before you—a captain's pension. You could live on to ninety; Dob's bound to make ninety. I'm the one wore-out, and I never left home.

DOB

Got any sense, you'll strike out for Utah.

NEAL

(Laughs) I'm no Mormon, couldn't stand all the wives.

DOB

Stayed too close to your mother; she burned you.

NEAL

(Nods) The main fault's mine—I didn't die young. Some men,

Dob, are born to be boys; and there for a while, I was one splendid boy.

As Neal continues, Porter mimes boredom with the old complaint.

Neal sees him, half-smiles but continues.

NEAL

At nineteen, see, I ought to just dropped. I've been as much use as a dick in church.

DOB

I used mine in church.

PORTER

I need to hear this.

DOB

Too awful to tell.

NEAL

Come on.

DOB

It was Wednesday night prayer-meeting. I was fourteen years old—

Cody has begun his return to the kitchen, stopping briefly to look in his parents' bedroom door and seeing Taw asleep. He moves on to the kitchen.

PORTER

You look a lot cooler.

CODY

That uniform's good for arctic raids only. You ready, Mr. Watkins?

PORTER

Cody, stop by the drugstore and get what I told you.

NEAL

What's the big order, stud—a gross of rubbers?

PORTER

A mild analgesic, if you truly must know—for my pitiful piles.

NEAL

Ruined *my* lunch.

Dob rises carefully and shakes Neal's hand.

DOB

You won't get her back. Or see her like. *(When Neal looks down)* Come see me one night. I still got some records you might need to hear—sweet music by the mile.

NEAL

A deal, Dob.

DOB

You won't. I forgive you. Just piss on my grave.

NEAL

I promise to *try*—my prostate's already tight as a virgin's.

DOB

Very few virgins I met had a prostrate. *(Note his pronunciation)*

Dob turns and shuffles slowly out the door.

Cody waves to his father.

NEAL

Your mother all right?

CODY

She's resting.

NEAL

Hurry back; I've barely seen you.

CODY

(At the door) I've barely changed. What's left'll be back in twenty minutes.

NEAL

Make it ten.

Cody leaves, shutting the door behind him

Porter eats the last forkful on his plate.

> PORTER

That was good potato salad. I forgot Taw could cook.

> NEAL

Some Baptist ladies brought that.

> PORTER

Better eat some; this'll be a long day.

> NEAL

Not for me, Captain. I'm quitting right now. You're the big local hero.

> PORTER

Hero? Of what?

> NEAL

(Waits) Strength and joy, to hear you tell it.

> PORTER

Just now, to Dob? That was harmless lies.

> NEAL

(Smiles but leans forward with his old avid interest) Let's talk like Neal and Porter of old. Lean back and howl. *(Throws his head back for a silent howl)*

> PORTER

A howl would just be one more lie. *(Waits)* I've had more life than you or me would ever have bet. You well know it took both Adolph Hitler and the Japanese air force to blast me out of here.

> NEAL

The raw truth now—I'm too tired for lies.

> PORTER

(Raises a hand to swear) Raw as a cut hand. I spent the first ten months pining for home. Nazi submarines might have been

flies for all I cared. *(Laughs)* Then one morning, we were in sight of England, my third safe crossing. I was on the fore-deck, counting seagulls, when one lone Messerschmidt fighter appeared. By the time I could think to save my ass, two shot boys lay between me and safety. *(Waits)*

NEAL

You managed to save them—

PORTER

I scuttled for cover. *(Waits)* They were screaming my name till the young one died. The other one quit and tried to sing— some Catholic hymn he didn't get to finish.

NEAL

Sad luck all round.

PORTER

(Laughs gently) Best luck I'd had. I got something bigger than home and you to moan about, so in my mind I signed on for life.

Neal studies him closely, then goes for the truth.

NEAL

What was I to you? *(When Porter frowns)* Back then, the dark ages, when we were good.

PORTER

You don't want to know. *(Waits)* But I may want to tell you. I thought I needed to serve Neal Avery, right–to–the–grave.

NEAL

Soul and body?

PORTER

(Faces Neal) Absolutely, you knew well as me. *(Laughs)* Is anybody now as *dumb* as I was, here at this table forty years back?

NEAL

(Smiles) And down on the river, under the stars.

PORTER

(Waits, then mildly) I was trying to save us both, best I could.

NEAL

From what?

PORTER

Tarnish, maybe—I meant you to *shine*. Maybe from life—exhaustion, change.

NEAL

(A long wait, looking down) Maybe you saved us. Our hearts still beat; we're the same two fools. *(Faces Porter)* I hope somebody's been better for you than Neal ever was.

PORTER

(Laughs gently) Soul *and* body? I've entertained my skin, very nicely—leave it at that. I've found needy gents that let me use my missionary skills—they could watch their faces, close, in my two eyes and see they counted for something on Earth.

NEAL

But nobody stayed—

PORTER

(Waits) Not a goddamned one—if I wanted that: I used to wonder. Course I get a ton of Christmas cards—pictures of toothy wives and kids, some named for me. *(Waits)* Mostly my soul's been locked in the freezer.

NEAL

You're not bitter though.

PORTER

I've tried to be. *(Laughs)* But hell, the freezer is crowded, friend. I don't lack company.

NEAL

Think you could come back and thaw my soul?—this body's long gone. *(When Porter delays)* You coming home?

PORTER

It's one of the cards in a mighty weak hand.

NEAL

Hearty thanks— *(Ambushed by a yawn)*

PORTER

You need sleep.

NEAL

Not yet. What's wrong with home?

PORTER

I'm wondering, hard. But first, you've missed way too much
sleep.

NEAL

Mother needed me, every breath. Then the wait for Cody.
(Shakes his head) I'm seeing strange things.

PORTER

For instance?

NEAL

For a start, how *rough* death is. *(An odd half-laugh)*

PORTER

You always said it was easy as diving, all your hourly suicide
threats.

NEAL

I'd never seen death.

PORTER

You held your father—

NEAL

He needed to go. Mother fought death like a spitting cobra.
(Waits) You serious with Dob? You mean to retire?

PORTER

I wasn't sure till I looked at Cody. That boy's eyes shook me.
(When Neal nods) Have you really talked to him?

NEAL

Didn't get here till four this morning. Then he slept till ten.
You've heard more than me.

PORTER

He's in bad trouble. He loves that war. *(When Neal fails to respond) You're* all right?

NEAL

I mostly quit my life-long howl. I just sit here and take what comes. *(Waits)* I'll have to say it *comes.*

PORTER

You repaid your mother for all she gave.

NEAL

You're kind to say so. Everybody else thinks I've been a martyr. But let me tell you, I got more fun out of Mother's mean mouth than all the comedies Hollywood made.

PORTER

Just this last Christmas I crept upstairs and tapped at her door. She said "Porter Farwell, explain yourself through that oak door." I knew she meant I'd forgot her birthday. I told her how busy I'd been, running Vietnam from a Navy office.

So she finally said "Step in. I can spare three minutes, but a war's no excuse to neglect the woman that washed your britches for five long years." I wrote to her once a week from that day on.

NEAL

I read them to her. She'd line them out on the air with a long blue finger, and of course she'd quarrel with most of your claims — "Porter's *lying* as ever."

The night she died, she made Taw leave the room — just me. Then she gave me exact directions for her funeral — a cheap pinebox so she'd turn to dirt fast, all black pallbearers, no sermon, no songs, just St. Paul's promise of a spiritual body.

She knew it by heart and got it all out, with no breath at all — "For this corruptible must put on incorruption, this mortal must put on immortality."

I was sobbing like a baby when she got to the end. Then she said "Porter Farwell was your great mistake." I said "Beg your pardon?" She said "Porter cherished you more than me." I said "Taw loves me; I think Cody does."

She actually *spat*, just missed my face. Then she said "Porter Farwell would have died for you." I said "I believe you but I never asked him to." She said "You asked *me* and I'm dying for you now."

PORTER

(A long wait) She was gone by then; she didn't mean it.

NEAL

She was clear as a perfect diamond that instant. I tried to laugh and I said "Please don't." I never in my life meant *anything* the way I meant that *please*. She didn't speak again but shook her head. And she died in two minutes—

Suddenly Neal surrenders to grief. He slumps on himself and covers his face.

Porter waits a long moment, then silently rises and moves to Neal.

Neal rises and steps into Porter's arms, a childlike hug.

Porter returns to his place at the table.

PORTER

(Waits again) You want me back?

NEAL

At the store? We're over-handed—

PORTER

In this house, your life?

NEAL

This house is about to be locked and abandoned.

PORTER

Why? It's a beauty, just needs a little paint.

NEAL

Taw made that announcement half an hour ago.

PORTER

(Smiles) Miss Roma shed no ray of love on Taw.

NEAL

These past three years though, they really got on. I'd come in some nights and hear them upstairs laughing like girls. They both understood we were up a back alley that lasted so long and then had a stop.

PORTER

The alley's ended. Lead Taw on out.

NEAL

Where to, please? I'm no millionaire. I manage the smallest store in a chain of menswear owned by gentlemen-Jews from Memphis. I'm a salaried hand; the little I've saved is waiting for Cody.

PORTER

Taw's salaried too.

NEAL

She all but pays *them* for the right to teach ancient history to modern thugs. One boy called her "cunt" two weeks ago.

PORTER

Your mother owned those miles of timber.

NEAL

Her illness ate the timber like beetles.

PORTER

Did she have a will?

NEAL

You remember her will — she'd call Sam Gibbs twice a month, writing one more of us in or out. Any will that's left won't stand up in a gentle breeze if somebody sues us.

PORTER

(A sudden new tack) You feel like a ride?

NEAL

Cody's getting your medicine —

PORTER

Let's ride down and ask Sam to open the will.

NEAL

Porter, let up a minute.

PORTER

I leave tonight.

NEAL

If you're in her will, I'll call you first thing.

PORTER

I want this house.

NEAL

Sir?

PORTER

Sell me this house.

NEAL

For what—firewood?

PORTER

I mean to come back; I'll need a good house.

NEAL

You've had a sunstroke.

PORTER

I'm cool as this glass. *(Touches Dob's tea)* I'm a Navy captain that earned his rank; I think I know how to make decisions.

NEAL

(Waits, then laughs) It *would* solve problems.

PORTER

(Standing) Let's read that will.

NEAL

It feels too quick.

PORTER

You'll think it's quick if it happens this year. I fly out of Raleigh at ten tonight.

NEAL

(Waits) Let me go tell Taw.

PORTER

Let's surprise her.

NEAL

At least wait for Cody.

PORTER

We'll pass Cody in the road; tell him then. If we wait much longer, Sam'll be locked in with that secretary he's napped with for years—*dictation* indeed!

Neal slowly stands, moves to the bedroom door and checks on Taw. Pure silence.

Porter mouths "Let's go" and points outside.

Neal shakes his head but slowly turns. They silently leave.

2

Immediately after. Deep shade moves across the house and a new light rises on Taw in bed. She rises, smooths the cover, finds a cotton housedress and slips it on.

TAW

The main thing I harp on with children is courtesy. I know it's old-fashioned. Even the babes now walk through a world that calls for switchblades more often than smiles.

But I keep believing I owe them at least a *message* from the past—the way people lived when they knew their neighbors and could lie down to rest and not fear rape and abduction down an interstate to a rusty dumpster where your corpse is flung, headfirst and stripped. I try to show them calm sane manners, and every year or so one of them thanks me.

So how could I beat on Neal like I did?—clawing at his

mother, who died in pain and was after all the soul that loved him since his first breath. The fact that she dreaded me no longer counts. She's gone and the pair of us are free to be everything we promised each other, pent up here.

Yet I lay there this past half-hour, and I could not think of a way to live here. I deeply believe in spirits of the dead. As an orphan I had to, just to believe love even existed. I can't wait in these walls to see Neal's mother strengthen on our blood and press back on us, for good or ill.

I was mean but right; I was true to myself. I can't stay here and — Jesus! — I won't. I'll flee for my life. I'm no old woman; I mean to last. I've got things to give — wonderful gifts — still waiting to *serve*.

Think of the flowers locked in one seed, that small and dry. That's me — that dry, that ready to thrive.

At the end of that, the light in the house returns to normal — again the natural summer changes of sun and shade. Taw stands on, quietly buttoning her dress.

The sound of a car approaching the backyard. Footsteps toward the door and Cody enters with a small paper bag which he sets on the counter. Then he swiftly moves to his parents' bedroom, creeps to Taw's back and embraces her suddenly.

Taw is pleasantly startled and laughs.

Cody lifts her and swings a turn in the air.

CODY

You were sawing wood when I crept out.

TAW

I was just meditating — becoming a Hindu in my middle years; it's my last hope.

CODY

For what?

> TAW

Oh the chance to return as a bird in my next life.

Cody lays his bag down and goes to the counter, tasting several bowls with his fingers.

Taw smilingly fends him off.

> CODY

You chosen which bird?

> TAW

It won't be a kiwi; I'll have wide wings. I mean to spend my next life soaring.

> CODY

Sounds like a buzzard.

> TAW

Wouldn't like the diet.

> CODY

An eagle.

> TAW

Too mean.

> CODY

No, you'd make a first-rate eagle—a golden raptor gliding toward sunset, both eyes scanning the ground for supper.

> TAW

The lady thanks you. Let her fix you a plate; then you go sleep.

Taw starts toward the kitchen.

Cody follows.

> CODY

Some food would be fine. If I fall face down in the jello, don't worry—half my soul's in southeast Asia.

Cody sits at the table.

Taw fills a plate, sets it before him, leans to kiss the crown of his hair, then sits beside him and studies his face.

TAW

I still don't believe they let you come home.

CODY

My commanding officer called me in, sat me down and said "How much did you love your grandmother?" I said "She's my third favorite thing on Earth." He said "She *wuz*." Then he said "Go home." Red Cross made the arrangements from there.

TAW

That was the truth—your third favorite thing?

CODY

(Faces her, unblinking, and waits) I just said so.

TAW

You know that pains me?

CODY

I do. I'm sorry.

TAW

You know your grandmother wanted me *gone*?

CODY

I well knew that.

TAW

And still you loved her?

CODY

I love her this instant.

TAW

(Smiles) Which means your ma can like it or lump it?

CODY

(Smiles also) There's room for you. I'm a fair-sized boy.

TAW

You're a man. Am I one of the blessed three?

CODY

I told you that before I could talk.

TAW

Want to tell me the order—first or second?

CODY

Hot irons couldn't prize it out of my heart.

TAW

How *is* your heart?

CODY

My pulse has slowed every month I've been gone.

TAW

Can you explain that?

CODY

I found my work.

TAW

Making orphans, burning homes?

CODY

(A long look at her eyes) That was Grandmother's tack; never thought you'd take it.

TAW

I watch the news; I've memorized your letters.

CODY

(Firm but calm) Quote where I kill or burn one thing.

TAW

The men you work with are doing it this minute.

CODY

That's not a quote.

TAW

The world knows it though.

CODY

The world caused all this nightmare I'm in.

TAW

And you're going back?

CODY

No choice. Two weeks' leave; they haul me back.

TAW

Against your will?

CODY

Not really, no ma'm.

TAW

We know you're brave. What will you prove?

CODY

Mainly how little I want to get shot.

TAW

But you'll head *toward* the guns.

CODY

—Shot for desertion. I take commands, Mother. I will till I've served my time or am dead.

Taw's hand goes quickly out and covers his mouth.

Cody accepts the gag for a moment, then pulls away.

CODY

Believe it. It could happen.

TAW

You talk like you want it. Son, you'd kill us both if you vanished.

CODY

(*Smiles*) Not you, never you. When they put Grandmother in the sod just now, you moved right up to the championship— strongest girl left.

TAW

I'm not glad of that. It would just mean years of pain to wade through. If anything serious happened to you, your father would break like ice in a bucket.

CODY

He outlasted Grandmother. That says a lot.

TAW

Pity got him through that. You're what he loves.

CODY

I love him—kindest man on Earth.

TAW

(Laughs) Kindest father, strongest mother—you're a lucky man. Any chance you'll be coming back here to live?

CODY

Wherever I've gone, whoever I've gone with, the *place* is strange—maybe good but strange. Let me step off a bus *here*, my feet know they're home. *(Waits)* And you and Father know I love you, but you know you cast more shade than I can grow in.

I can't sell men's cheap ready-to-wear; I can't teach school.

Mother, all these safe clean lovable towns are dead, cold *dead*. Nobody under fifty, with a normal IQ, can make a fair living in such a kind place.

TAW

(Waits, then nods) I hate it but I know it's true. My few good pupils streak for the light—some city that'll pay them and grind them to filthy dust, in no time.

CODY

(Smiles) So if I leave Vietnam with all my parts and go to a city, I'll be filthy powder in no time fast?

TAW

You just get out, with every part. Then we'll worry about the rest.

CODY

Will Dad understand?

TAW

(Nods) He has, for years. Course it's breaking his heart. You've been the thing that never failed him.

CODY

I've failed him far more times than you know; he just hasn't seen it.

TAW

Me either. So don't tell me now. I live in the hope you may turn out to be *the* person who makes it to perfect.

CODY

You're a schoolteacher, Mother. You know better.

TAW

It's *why* I'm a teacher. Teachers live on hope—that one child makes it, all the way on out and *there*.

CODY

Perfect as God—

TAW

(Smiles) I didn't say that.

CODY

Christ did. "Be ye perfect as your Father in Heaven."

TAW

Christ *was* a high-minded boy. I've often rejoiced I didn't teach him. Life was easier then though.

CODY

Life anytime is harder than hell.

TAW

And you've been to Hell.

CODY

You asking a question?

TAW

Confirming a fact.

CODY

I look that bad?

TAW

You want to know?

CODY

I'm *your* blood son; I guess I can bear it.

TAW

You look very much like you've been in a kiln, baked for a year in white-hot fire.

CODY

You been watching too much TV.

TAW

I been watching *you*, since the day you were born.

CODY

There've been a few four-day really rough patches.

TAW

Any possible way not to go back?

CODY

You could shoot me this minute. *(Waits)* I want to go back.

TAW

I can't say I understand how that can be. You mourned a week when your hamster died.

CODY

I wish I could tell you. I can't. But I crave it.

TAW

What part, Cody? Why?

CODY

(Waits, then rises and begins to speak as he prowls the room— lightly brushing objects, tasting foods, ending at the sink where he washes his hands) The power, all the power. I know it's a risky hunger and must stop before I can come back anywhere near anybody I love. But for now out there, I'm very near perfect. I make a choice. I give the order. My men trust me. They proceed to obey.

We're all still alive too; I've yet to lose one. And we've been through thirty-six firefights. Been out four days with no drop of water but what hot dew we could lick off leaves. Been so close to death we could count every purple vein in his eye. But I brought them all in.

I've yet to fail, not that far from home. I know I won't.

TAW

Never say *won't*.

CODY

(Shakes his head) I won't fail *there*—I know: not *there*. It's somehow been shown to me in the night.

TAW

You're not having visions?

CODY

Not drugs now, easy. No, I've just waked up night after night and heard my own voice talk to itself. It just says "Never fear, never flinch. Stand up and step onward."

Cody dries his hands slowly.

TAW

Maybe you've already lost your mind.

CODY

(Waits) I'm who I've been since the day you made me. I just found the place my whole body *works*.

TAW

Then you can't come back.

CODY

Not as me. I already told you.

TAW

You won't try to die?

CODY

I mean to be back. Most people last; that's strangest of all.

TAW

You can't know how this punishes me.

CODY

For what?

TAW

—What I wanted. I wanted you, since I was a girl, long before I met your father. I wanted a healthy boy in working order, with a strong clear face that could last a whole life—outlast me, not vanish, not flee, not fall down begging help from others. I got my whole wish and—son—it burns.

CODY

(Waits) I can't help you now. I hope some day you can ease up and love me.

TAW

If I loved you any harder, I'd fry us both crisp.

CODY

You may have already—you and Dad together. I may well be charred past recognition.

TAW

I'd know your eyes on the back of the moon.

CODY

That's where I've *been*. And am going back.

TAW

Bless—your—heart. *(Waits)* Bless—your—*hide*. What else can I say?

A knock at the yard door. Cody looks to Taw, then quickly bends to kiss her hand.

Taw nods and signs him to open the door.

CODY

Virginia. Well, good.

VIRGINIA

I couldn't quit work in time for the funeral; but this is my lunch, so I thought I'd see if you really got back.

CODY

I did and it's hot as anywhere else but you're welcome in.

Taw stands in place and smiles toward Virginia.

Virginia walks past Cody, then stops halfway between him and the table. She turns and studies him carefully.

CODY

You know me?

VIRGINIA

Almost. You've changed some—here. *(Strokes at her eyes)*

CODY

It's bright out there.

VIRGINIA

I lost my sunglasses.

CODY

Didn't mean the *sun.*

Virginia is puzzled and embarrassed.

CODY

I meant my present line of work—strong glare, day and night. *(Suddenly points)* Southeast Asia.

VIRGINIA

(Slowly) So I've heard. *(Faces Taw)* Afternoon, Mrs. Avery.

TAW

(Nods and smiles) Gin, we've hardly seen you.

VIRGINIA

I keep pretty busy. In the Welfare Department.

TAW

That must be thrilling.

VIRGINIA

(Smiles) Mainly sad.

TAW

Let me fix you some lunch.

VIRGINIA

No thanks. I meant to bake you some blueberry muffins; but then I got stuck on a case last evening, way out in the sticks —

TAW

You watch yourself, riding alone out there in the dark.

VIRGINIA

I carry my pistol. *(Holds up her purse)* Course I'd dread to use it.

TAW

Use it please. Ask questions later.

CODY

You're taking a hard new line, *Ms.* Avery.

TAW

So is life, around here at least.

VIRGINIA

One of the girls that works with me was trapped last week by three grown men in a trailer by the river —

TAW

You two sit down and make yourselves easy. I need to start on the thank-you notes.

CODY

(Slowly to Taw) Sit still; let me watch you.

TAW

You memorized me twenty-eight years ago. I need to work; it'll soothe my nerves.

VIRGINIA

I'm sorry, Mrs. Avery. But I guess it was a blessing.

TAW

Thank you. It was time.

CODY

Death's no kind of blessing — on anybody, ever.

TAW

Thank *you*, son. You need rest too.

CODY

I'll be on up after while.

Taw leaves the hall door ajar behind her.

Cody waits a moment, then shuts the door quietly.

Virginia moves toward the table to sit.

Cody meets her in the midst of the room, takes both her hands, studies her face. Then he kisses her slowly but lightly on the neck.

When he stands back, Virginia pauses briefly, then goes to the table and sits.

Cody remains standing.

CODY

You look mighty fine. I guess I forgot.

VIRGINIA

Not for lack of my news.

CODY

Your letters have gone a long way to save me.

VIRGINIA

I'm glad to know it. It's been a little like talking to a statue.

CODY

I'm sorry. But when I finish a day out there, the last thing I need is to lie on wet ground and relive it on paper.

VIRGINIA

You might send a postcard every two or three weeks—just a big check mark to show you're well.

CODY

A deal. I'll try.

VIRGINIA

It's not a deal, Cody. We don't have a *deal.*

CODY

And you don't mind?

Virginia waits to think.

Cody moves to the table and sits beside her.

VIRGINIA

I mind something awful. But I'm not waiting, no.

CODY

Can't ask you to. I'm still way out in the Asian air on a hot steel tether; whether I die or lose a few legs is the pressing issue.

VIRGINIA

I said I understood. I'm a full-grown woman with 20/20 eyes; I choose my path.

CODY

But it runs toward me.

VIRGINIA

It wants to, yes. It always has.

CODY

We haven't touched in — what? — two years.

VIRGINIA

I've missed it but touch isn't *all.*

CODY

Gin, I've missed your body like food. Very few nights pass that I don't wake at the end of a dream where I've prowled your body and torn you *up.*

VIRGINIA

(Smiles) I don't know whether to thank you or run.

CODY

It's me owes the thanks. But sure, *you* run.

VIRGINIA

I've known a few others, and some were good men. But you're the main actor in my dreams too.

CODY

Tell me the plot; I need to rehearse.

VIRGINIA

(Waits) I don't tear you up. You get light duties—peaceful walks through the woods. We float in your old skiff on the river.

CODY

What's my first line?

VIRGINIA

You don't say a word.

CODY

Not ever? Just dumb?

VIRGINIA

Peaceful. Still. You do get to smile, from various angles— above and below.

Cody puts his face through a series of smiles, subtle to comic.

VIRGINIA

The first smile's what I dream about—calm and looking straight at my eyes.

CODY

In endless gratitude?

VIRGINIA

(Waits) I never once asked you for thanks, just devotion.

CODY

I'm sorry; you're right. But devotion is something for my next life, if I get a next life. I can't plan it now.

VIRGINIA

Are you really that special—postponing happiness to punish us both? Not risking yourself?

CODY

I *risk* myself. A full set of limbs, all pink and moving, at the end of a day is all I pray for yet awhile.

VIRGINIA

Me too, on the back roads of this poor county. I go in shacks that make your tent look like the Waldorf with dual exhausts. I go to give money, and even then I face down men that had just as soon cut my throat as spit.

CODY

Forget my future and plan yourself a safer life.

VIRGINIA

The only reason to go that far would be the certainty we won't want each other, ever again.

CODY

You said it, not I.

VIRGINIA

I didn't say anything certain yet. When I do, it'll be this— Cody, I want you. I want you for good, even if you die next Wednesday noon, half the world away. Or come back here with pieces missing.

CODY

(Waits) Gin, I can thank you; but I can't match that—not for anybody now.

VIRGINIA

Then say the next thing.

CODY

You say it for me.

VIRGINIA

I don't love you.

CODY

Is that good enough? Have I got to repeat it?

VIRGINIA

For the record, please.

CODY

Virginia–Wilson–I–don't–love–you. Not now. Maybe nevermore.

VIRGINIA

Is there somebody else?

CODY

No, thank God.

VIRGINIA

Was there ever any love, at all, in these twelve years?

CODY

Has it been that long?

VIRGINIA

Just since eleventh grade.

CODY

Just? I've been to the moon since then.

VIRGINIA

No. Some astronauts did—and hit golf balls and came home
grinning like chimpanzees. You went to State College, then
came back here, tried to work with your father, then joined the
Marines. That's not quite the moon.

CODY

Then I can't tell you.

VIRGINIA

Help me understand.

CODY

If I did—and I could—you'd run and not stop till you hit
Vermont.

VIRGINIA

I can take it.

CODY

I won't give it.

VIRGINIA

So I might as well leave?

CODY

(Nods) Please.

VIRGINIA

For good?

CODY

(Waits, laughs) You really do wolf down the pain—

VIRGINIA

Till I know I'm full.

CODY

(Studies her face) You're full to the eyes. I can't stay here much longer and watch you.

Virginia takes up her bag from the floor; then she stands in place. At no point does she weaken or break.

Cody stays still but continues to watch her.

VIRGINIA

I'm sorry your grandmother didn't get to see you.

CODY

She saw me, back when I was good to see.

VIRGINIA

You're good right now, but you're young and tired.

CODY

I'm old as rocks in the Blue Ridge mountains and twice as tired.

Virginia walks briskly to the yard door, opens it wide.

VIRGINIA

I shouldn't send letters?

CODY

(Smiles) Mail's always welcome with our boys abroad.

VIRGINIA

Say it again—you don't love me.

CODY

(Shakes his head) That minute's gone by.

VIRGINIA

(Waits) I'll see you when you're back.

CODY

(Shuts his eyes, smiles) When I'm *back*.

Virginia turns and leaves; the door shuts behind her.

Cody stays at the table; his eyes stay shut. Like a blind man, he feeds himself an awkward mouthful—missing his lips, then finding the hole.

3

Immediately after. The light in the kitchen alters as it had at the start of Scene 2—first an alternation of sun and shade, then a general darkness with only Cody lit. When he has chewed his last mouthful of food, he wipes at his lips with the back of a hand. His cheeks are smeared. Then he stands in place—hands on the table—and strains to speak to the audience.

CODY

You. I can make you understand. Nobody here but me and you. The moon—I went to the actual moon, not the dry-gulch country club the astronauts played on.

The place I went to is not that far. The air's not a whole lot hotter than here; the land itself's lovely—vague like the dream where you're always alone but happy in a flat-bottomed boat, steady on a brown stream barely forging through narrow banks with high green leaves and drifts of dragonflies, butterflies, moths. The first few weeks I thought it was fine.

Then one night I got sent with some men in the light of

nothing but phosphorus flares, and we got hit by incoming hell so fast I knew I was bound to die. When I came to, I'd flown ten yards and was on my back, waiting for my lungs to start.

I felt like something was wrong with my legs, and I dreaded to look. It was too dark to see, but I reached down slow; and there were my knees and upper shins. I thought "Anyhow I've got my legs." Then I reached for my feet, and my hands drew back all gummed with a hot wet mess that moved. I thought "Cody-Boy, this could have been worse. They'll teach you to walk on your two strong stumps."

But it was worse. The hot wet mess was my friend Phil, Phil Wilkerson. The dome of his brain was sprayed on my boots, the rest of him lay there just past reach. It still made sounds, some high little whine like a far-off siren or a female cat, reamed for the tenth time under the stars in your back alley. I got up then and tried to collect what I could of Phil, just seizing my way with my hands in the dark.

I can almost make you understand. I can try to let you in at my heart, in here where it's trapped under all this cloth. I can swear I know things you need to hear. I can show you ways to the actual moon. *(Slowly begins unbuttoning his shirt and ends by showing his bare chest, neck to navel. His voice and tone deepen in force, but at no point does he lose an uncanny self-possession)*

Thick night—flares—scalded stars—grass sharp as knives at body heat—crawling leaves—dirt—teeth in the blood—scraps of teeth—wet warm splinters of bone in your hand—

You will never get back—if you do, you will sit here sealed like a tomb, the absolute perfect unbreachable tomb—like me—like Phil sprayed hot on my boots—

At your mother's tit—warm milk on your tongue—slow down your throat—she takes you gently by the weak pink heels and flings you time after time at the wall till all that's left is the rags of you screaming—and no help comes—no help exists—you are on the moon—no father, grandmother, sheriff or kin—the ac-

tual moon—it is not that far from where we wait this instant—I
can take you—

*Cody slowly begins to button his shirt, then tucks it in neatly.
Light begins to resume in the kitchen—a gradual varying
sunlight and shade. When the room is normal, Cody goes to the
hall door, opens it, walks through and shuts it behind him.*

ACT TWO

1

Two-thirty in the afternoon, Roma Avery's kitchen. The room is unchanged since Cody's departure at the end of Act One. The hall door opens and Taw walks in, still in her cotton dress. She takes the dishes from table to sink and begins drawing hot water to soak them.

Cody is visible, asleep in his room.

The yard door opens. Neal and Porter walk in, both plainly affected by the heat of the day.

TAW

Middle-aged men, with indoor jobs, should have better sense than to brave this day.

PORTER

So right.

Neal goes to Taw, kisses her neck, then goes to the table and sits.

Porter watches the kiss, then also sits.

TAW

Where've you been?

NEAL

Sam Gibbs'. To read Mother's will.

TAW

You saw your mother's will three months ago, when she called Sam up here for that last codicil.

NEAL

I led Sam upstairs but Mother made me leave.

TAW

You didn't tell me—

Porter suddenly lays his head on the table and bursts out laughing.

Neal tries to resist but then joins in. They both share a note of desperate glee.

TAW

You're about to tell me she left every cent to one of those mangy hounds she kept.

Porter turns to Neal for the answer.

Neal smiles on in silence.

PORTER

Almost. No, she set up a fund for the simplification of American spelling and punctuation—administered by me.

TAW

Porter, please.

PORTER

I'm suffering sunstroke.

Taw dries her hands and leans on the sink, facing Neal.

Neal tries to avoid her eyes but finally relents.

NEAL

She left me five thousand in stocks. She left you ten thousand dollars cash, with a nice long statement of perpetual thanks. The rest now belongs to our fortunate son.

TAW

Cody? How much?

NEAL

Sam's working that up. Safe to say though—young Cody's *rich*. He owns this house and all Mother's land, her stocks and bonds, even my father's farm.

TAW

And you're surprised?

NEAL

(Waits) I don't know. Maybe. I sure didn't move in here to win money, and God Himself couldn't foretell Mother. But sure, I guess I feel a little stunned. I thought she trusted me.

TAW

Stunned? Ten thousand dollars to me? I may keel over.

NEAL

I always said she respected you; you stood up to her.

TAW

I didn't know it earned me a Mercedes Benz.

NEAL

Plainly it did. Sam's sending you a copy of the grateful clause, suitable for framing.

TAW

What else did she say?

NEAL

Not much. Said Cody Avery was perfect. *(To Porter)* How did she put it?

PORTER

She said "Cody Avery has not given less than complete satisfaction."

Taw smiles, comes to the table and sits. Then she also laughs.

NEAL

(Smiling) Why are you laughing? We're out in the *street*.

TAW

I'm laughing for joy. We're free as fleas.

PORTER

Call that old girlfriend of Cody's at the welfare office; she'll find you a dry pup tent by winter. Course you'll need food stamps—dried beans, rolled oats, beef hearts: you'll love it!

TAW

We can take a long trip—maybe rent us a cottage this fall at the beach—then come back here and find a new house.

NEAL

School opens in the fall—

TAW

Late summer then. We can move any day.

PORTER

You've got the down-payment, between you at least.

TAW

Call Genevieve's brother—now. *(When Neal shakes his head)* I'm serious; this has got to be fate.

NEAL

Fate saw to it I was born in this house—

TAW

So was your mother; so are ten zillion termites an hour. Cody's managed a war half the world away; I guess he can handle this tired old wreck.

NEAL

He won't live here. Take a look at his eyes.

TAW

I'm his mother; I made him. *I* can't read his eyes. Cody may come back—Virginia Wilson paid a call just now.

NEAL

He won't want Virginia.

TAW

Has he told you that?

NEAL

I haven't had a minute with Cody.

PORTER

Where's he gone?

TAW

Upstairs, to sleep.

PORTER

If he's not up soon, I'll need to rouse him. *(When Taw and Neal study him)* I've got a proposition he needs to hear. *(Lets them lean toward him)* I want this house.

NEAL

Get your head tested, Porter.

PORTER

My head got tested three weeks ago. I'm the sanest soul on the eastern seaboard. And running a war from a desk in Norfolk is too tame for me. I'm taking your dare and coming home. I want this house, if Cody'll sell it.

NEAL

You don't need this.

PORTER

The hell I don't. I loved this house; I honored your mother.

TAW

But it's huge, old friend. You'd rattle like buckshot.

PORTER

I need to rattle. I've been pent up in ships and pigeonholes. Here I can spread out, stretch—I might grow. Might even learn a trade for my golden years—make fine guitars.

NEAL

Before you could build a musical comb, you'd need to pitch in and save this place.

TAW

I doubt you could save it—you *and* your combs.

PORTER

Look, if you two want me not to live here, say the word. But if all you're saying is, the place needs work, I can move back and put my shoulder to it.

NEAL

You can't drive a nail.

PORTER

I've saved good money for thirty years. I can buy help to prop up the pyramids. But answer my question—would you mind me here?

Taw nods back to Neal.

NEAL

The house is not mine, friend. Don't ask me.

PORTER

You'd speak to me though?

NEAL

(Smiles and nods) Wouldn't visit you much. Course you could track me down in my tent.

PORTER

Come as far as the porch; sit and drink gin with me.

NEAL

(Waits) It's no joke to me. I couldn't come near.

TAW

Your mother knew we didn't want this.

NEAL

She never asked me. Maybe I was too busy hauling her bedpans or washing her drawers.

TAW

You never washed a stitch. The laundry I've put out of this very room would stretch on a line from here to Samoa.

NEAL

Don't play the fool; it makes you look coarse. I spared you more
filth than you ever dreamed.

TAW

(Calmer) You honored your mother to the end. Nobody faults
you.

NEAL

They will though. Guess how the town'll love this news—you
and me up here three years, swabbing shit, and Mother leaves
it all to a boy that never said more to her than "Hey" with a
boyish grin as he ran off to play.

TAW

Cody struck some cord she'd waited to hear—nobody else did.
I've known that always. *(When Neal looks adamant)* He's our
son, right? We're proud of him, aren't we?

NEAL

Proud? *(Waits, a genuine search for an answer)*

PORTER

I am. And I've known him long as you; I stood beside you the
first time you saw him. God made other babies that year, I'm
sure—they're out in the streets right now, sucking drugs—but
nobody got a finer child than Cody.

TAW

Thank you, friend.

Taw looks to Neal.

Neal accepts the look but his face stays blank.

TAW

Please call Dillard and ask him his price; go that far at least.

NEAL

Our perfect boy just may realize he needs caretakers.

TAW

(Waits) I've said what I've got to say about that. *(Stands)* And now I'm going to the grocery store.

PORTER

You've got food for six more weeks.

TAW

People mean to be kind, but they leave out *staples.* And believe it or not, I need the air.

PORTER

Let me be your bag-boy. *(Begins to stand)*

TAW

I'll manage; stay cool.

PORTER

I need air too.

Taw nods and moves toward the yard door.

Porter follows her, then pauses at the door.

PORTER

(To Neal) What can I bring you?

NEAL

Not a thing they sell.

PORTER

You want me to stay?

NEAL

Thank you, no.

Taw leaves.

Porter follows and shuts the door behind him.

Neal sits motionless till they are well gone. He loosens his tie, then tugs it off and drops it to the floor.

2

Immediately after. The light shifts to an unnatural radiance that settles on Neal. He sits at the table; but as feeling mounts, he paces the entire room, touching objects he has known all his life.

NEAL

This house has brought me about as much happiness as Hong Kong flu, so why is one more aging boy steadily moaning to stay in place? Fact is, I'm far enough on in my little trip to see the end up there on the hill—the houses and chimneys of death and then what?—and I think I can make you a list of my deeds so you'll understand.

I honored my mother, who was mean but funny. I've been more than normally true to my wife, though she's not exactly beaming contentment. I never got round to building a woodshed, much less a house. So the world won't recall Neal Avery the Builder—no park, no monument, no corporation. I did trip Taw into making a son that has caused less grief than most sons lately.

On Judgment Day I'll take my stand on Cody Avery's ample shoulders, a strong good man I trust entirely. Cody of course is aching to finish a war dumb and vicious as any child's game. But he owns this house. He'll want it like you want the middle-aged mumps. He'll sell it to Porter, who'll come back and find the town so changed he'll beg to croak and return as one great termite to eat it.

(Paradoxically, his voice and face begin to lighten till—at the end—he has half-cheered himself) So I hate the future. I love my wife but she needs me like the Mexican itch. What I want is to hole up alone in these thick walls till the trump of Doom and watch my son through these old windows—making his own path, renewing our line. I won't even ask to meet his wife, much less touch the children. *(Waits, then beams a lasting smile)*

I'm crazy as any tramp in the alley—pushing a dogcart, saving dead light-bulbs, eating lettuce from garbage cans. I could live in New York City under bridges in nights so cold the Hudson'll freeze. I'm that disappointed. But I don't want pity. I just want me alone in this house till we fall down, fall in, disappear.

Brace yourself—I've loved this world more than anyone else I know or see, from this standpoint. You can be torn as me and still beg life. Course I'd die this instant, in absolute torture, to save my son, who's very—nearly—lost—his—mind.

(Waits) I trust you'd die for a child of yours. If not, I'm sorry I said this much. Unless your son's the blind bigshot that's running this war. *(Waits)* Then take him please this message from me.

(Waits) Roll it, Big Bubba! Roll it *on!*

At the end Neal has stopped at the sink. He turns on the water, washes his face and wets his hair as light rises naturally. Finished, he doesn't dry himself but goes directly to Cody's room, leans silently over Cody's sleeping face and shakes water on him.

Cody wakes, startled, dresses quickly through the start of Scene 3 as he and Neal return to the kitchen.

3

Still in Cody's bedroom.

CODY

You drowning yourself?

NEAL

Just purging my sins away, away. *(Sings the final word on a long bass note)*

CODY

Will tap water do it?

NEAL

If it's cold enough.

CODY

Maybe I ought to just draw a big tub full and soak all week.

NEAL

(Smiles) Your soul's that tainted?

CODY

(Waits to think; then shakes his head and smiles) I can't start adding up those accounts till I'm home for good.

Cody begins to move toward the kitchen, Neal close behind.

NEAL

Where's home going to be?

CODY

Not you—Mother's already jumped me on that.

NEAL

(Goes to the table) I've got some news your mother lacked.

CODY

(Stays by the sink) Sir?

NEAL

You own this house.

CODY

Did Grandmother tell you?

NEAL

We opened the will at Sam Gibbs' office. You're far and away her main beneficiary—this house, miles of land, every cent of the money but fifteen thousand.

CODY

Which comes to you?

NEAL

(Laughs) Ten thousand to your mother; I get a small tip.

CODY

(Waits) This is one of her jokes.

NEAL

Meaner than most.

CODY

She's bound to have been incompetent.

NEAL

(A hushing finger to his lips) Don't let her ghost hear you. Roma Avery was clear-eyed as any bald eagle till the instant she died, stone-blind or not.

CODY

I want you to have it.

NEAL

She meant it for you, this house above all.

CODY

So I've owned it several days. Now it's yours and Mother's.

NEAL

(Shakes his head) Your mother is all but dumb with relief. She gave me an ultimatum at noon—she was leaving posthaste; I could follow if I liked.

CODY

(Looking around) I won't live here, if I ever come back.

NEAL

(Laughs) I always knew I missed a lot, not going to war. You and Porter make choices quick as I drink water. A woman that loved you like God loves light has died in pain; she left you a fortune. You lean on a kitchen sink and give it away, with not one worry but flat-out war ten thousand miles off, aimed right at your heart.

CODY

I'm as bad off as you. I can't have *things* on my back now.

NEAL

Then there won't be, son. Porter wants the house; he'll buy it tonight. I'll run the rest till you get home.

CODY

It won't be to this town—you understand.

NEAL

I do. It hurts to say it. *(When Cody waits)* I love you way past anybody else. I have ever since you were three days old.

CODY

(Laughs) How did I mess up the first two days?

NEAL

You didn't. But you waited till the third day to choose me. You were never breast-fed, see—that was out of style—so given the choice of my arms or Taw's, you'd mostly take mine.

CODY

(Waits) I'm a murderer, Dad. I've killed eighteen human beings, entirely against their will. And eighteen's just the number I know. Only God knows how many more in the night.

NEAL

That's nothing to me.

CODY

Your son's a trained killer—can't wait to lengthen his gory list.

NEAL

My son's obeying presidential orders.

CODY

The President's mad as a hatter on speed.

NEAL

That's not your fault—

CODY

It will be if God turns out to be real. Would you want to stand beside me at Judgment and face up to killing a girl—maybe ten—with her hands out toward you?

NEAL

I'm sure God can take it.

CODY

(Waits, laughs) He can sure-to-Christ dish it out.

Cody moves on to the table and sits.

NEAL

I wish I could help you.

CODY

You could. *(Waits)* Shoot me. *(When Neal frowns, Cody taps his own temple)* Right here; the skull's thin here.

NEAL

(Waits, then smiles) You got that mess from me—relax.

CODY

I'm serious.

NEAL

I thought I was. I've sat at this table, more than once in my life, and asked my mother to do me in—or watch me do it.

CODY

Who did you ever kill?

NEAL

Your mother, for a start—

CODY

Mother's strong as a bear in armor.

NEAL

She is. She hates it. I made her that hard. *(Waits)* You didn't know her back at the start. She was strong, all right, but beautiful too. No magnet ever pulled stronger than Taw.

CODY

So how did you harm her?

NEAL

Nailing her down, beside me and Mother. Making her swear in the presence of God to stay by a man that's sterile as a crowbar.

CODY

You saying I'm a bastard?

NEAL

No, you're mine. *(Waits)* Now you claim you're a killer. *(Smiles)* And that adds up to a sad damned sight—a weak-willed upright shadow like me pumping out a cold killer as his one big deed.

Cody rises suddenly.

CODY

You feel like a drink?

NEAL

I promised your mother—

CODY

Dad, you're *grown.* I'll run to the store.

Neal silently points to a cabinet.

Baffled, Cody goes, opens the door, finds a full fifth of bourbon and holds it up.

CODY

Whoa! Who's the bootlegger?

NEAL

Your mother, oddly. It's been there just a little more than three years.

CODY

But the seal's unbroken.

NEAL

The week we moved in here to watch Mother, Taw came home with one brown bag. I didn't say a word and that nearly killed her. Finally she thrust out the bag and said "If you need this at critical points, I'll understand." I laughed till dawn.

CODY

Sounds merciful to me.

NEAL

I didn't mind Mother. Almost to the end, she gave in return for my little service. Good jokes, long poems she learned as a girl and could say by the hour, memories of her own father—wild as a stag: a great deal else I hadn't heard.

CODY

I hope I don't have to wait long to hear it.

NEAL

At least not till I'm blind and stunned.

CODY

Tell the best one now.

NEAL

First, pour that drink.

CODY

And if Mother drives up?

NEAL

She gets to have a tantrum. Pour me one pure drink.

CODY

Virgin bourbon, with water?

NEAL

Straight in the glass—way we learned in Prohibition. We just used to tilt back and drink it like chickens.

Cody stands with the bottle, finds two glasses and pours long straight drinks, no ice. Then he comes to the table and sits.

CODY

You're the elder; you toast.

NEAL

(Waits) To Roma Avery, wherever she roams. To the fellow spirits who now get to meet her. Hold tight, old spirits; don't run back here! You'll grow to cherish her; it just takes time. *(Waits again, then takes a long swallow)*

CODY

Amen. *(Drinks)*

Neal faces Cody, smiles; then reaches with both hands, takes Cody's hands and bends to kiss them.

NEAL

Live where you need to. But come back *living.*

CODY

(Finally nods) Nobody's asked that much before. Since it's you, I'll do my best to obey.

NEAL

Then I'll die happy.

CODY

But no time soon?

NEAL

Oh no, I'm not rushing.

CODY

Then ease up and tell me about Grandmother, the secrets she told you. The best one first.

NEAL

(Waits) She found a gigolo when my father died.

CODY

Whoa here again!

NEAL

Not right away—she waited seven years. Then she went to Richmond on a shopping spree. She took a big room at the Jefferson Hotel—live alligators in a pond in the lobby.

The second night, she wore black velvet and went to dinner right by herself. Even then, in the forties, that was all but breathtaking—a lone respectable woman in public after sundown. Still the dinner went fine, with a live string band—oysters on the half-shell, softshell crabs and fruit compote.

Then she withdrew to the glorious lobby—a space that could

hold ancient Rome *and* Athens. She took out a thrilling book to read; but in no time, a young man stood up from playing bridge at a nearby table and came straight toward her — a 4-F like me, for mild heart murmurs.

She said he looked like Tyrone Power* but with St. Paul's eyes — that must have meant *hot*. He was dressed in an elegant black tuxedo; and he introduced himself as Fontaine Belfont — Washington and Lee, in the law school there. He offered his hand, she stood up and took it, he never broke stride. Just led her straight to the elevator, punched the button for her floor (he somehow knew), stopped right at her door, then held out his hand.

Not breaking silence, Miss Roma surrendered the key with a smile —

CODY

(Smiles) Ma's right; you shouldn't drink.

NEAL

(Empties his glass) I swear to St. Paul. Verbatim what your grandmother told me, not two months ago.

CODY

She didn't stop there?

NEAL

She was delicate, sure, but managed to give me an hour more. They ordered room service — Fontaine was hungry, a whole boiled lobster.

The sound of a car coming into the yard.

CODY

Jump to the end — did he spend the night?

NEAL

Four days and nights — and followed her home.

*Or, depending upon the actor who plays Fontaine, another romantic male star of the time — Leslie Howard, Gary Cooper, for instance.

CODY

To here?

NEAL

(Touches the table) This *spot.* I met him one morning at early breakfast. She introduced him as a man selling Bibles to pay his tuition.

The sound of steps approaching the yard door.

CODY

(Half-whispers) How long did it last?

NEAL

(Normal volume) I'm not sure—but years.

The yard door opens. Taw enters with a bag but neither man notices.

CODY

Sweet Jesus in tights!

TAW

No, just your mother in too hot a dress.

Cody rises to help her.

Taw gives him the bag, pauses to register the liquor bottle but proceeds to shelve the groceries—no comment.

Cody leans on a counter, leaving his half-full glass on the table.

With subdued defiance Neal takes the swallow that empties his glass.

NEAL

You lost Porter.

TAW

He ran into Baxter Capps and went off with him.

CODY

Where to?

NEAL

Those condominiums out by the quarry. Baxter owns two or three.

CODY

The granite quarry? *(Neal nods)* They ruined that too? If you don't need the car, let me drive out there.

NEAL

It's a pitiful sight.

Cody takes his mother's keys from the counter and opens the door.

CODY

I'll just find Porter and bring him right back.

Cody leaves.

Taw continues her shelving.

NEAL

Congratulations.

TAW

Thank you. *(Turns, smiling)* For what?

NEAL

You scared him to death—barging in on the liquor—but you brought it off like a Playboy Bunny.

TAW

I trust I've mellowed. *(Waits)* It's *mellow* or *rot*.

NEAL

Apparently so. Course we rot anyhow.

TAW

That's characteristic. *(Waits)* What did Cody say?

NEAL

We were recollecting Mother.

TAW

The will, I meant. How'd he take the news?

NEAL

Oh he went all to pieces, gave it all back to us. I politely refused.

TAW

Good. It'll help him come back safe.

NEAL

That's cloudy logic.

TAW

Knowing he's got a big fortune here—that'll draw him back.

NEAL

It won't work that way, Taw. Understand—Cody can't live here: *can't* and *won't*.

TAW

(Finished with the shelving, comes to the table and stands)
Ninety percent of all human beings live in the sound of their parents' voices.

NEAL

And hate ninety-nine percent of their days.

TAW

Just search any issue of the *National Geographic*—everybody's laughing in the door of their mud hut with toothless Mom and Dad in reach.

NEAL

Wake up. We're not in the Third World yet.

TAW

Any day though—the First World's a *goner*. Cody could be a pioneer, come back home and gather his clan like olden days.

NEAL

He won't. Get ready.

TAW

Did you tell him Porter wants this house?

NEAL

(Nods) Then we started drinking and Mother came up. I told him about her gigolo.

TAW

You didn't.

NEAL

Why not? It softens her memory, helps *me* love her more.

TAW

He didn't seem to mind?

NEAL

Our son has killed a few people, Taw. A little canoodling in the family tree's not likely to throw him.

TAW

His grandmother though—

NEAL

Now you're speaking for yourself—Priscilla Mullins, the Puritan Maid.

TAW

Any puritan maid teaching school now would die every day. *(Neal is listening but silent)* Miscarried babies in the girls' bathroom, too big to flush.

NEAL

That did it. I'll never eat again.

TAW

Can't ship Porter off without a big meal.

NEAL

What you planning?

TAW

Beefsteaks—I got five nice ones.

NEAL

Who's the fifth mouth?

TAW

Virginia Wilson, in case Cody asked her.

NEAL

Freeze *that* steak right now; I can tell you.

TAW

I'll let Cody tell me.

NEAL

Suit yourself; it'll spoil.

TAW

I'm planning to suit myself, more and more.

NEAL

That'll leave me out.

TAW

Remains to be seen.

Neal waits, chooses not to answer, then shudders.

TAW

You're not catching cold?

NEAL

No, just feeling the wind in my face. *(A half-comic imitation of age)* —A stunned old man holed up here alone.

TAW

Neal Avery, I've loved you two-thirds of my life. Nothing's likely to make me change the habit

NEAL

Then I've loved you.

TAW

I don't doubt that.

NEAL

Are you glad?

TAW

Glad? I think so—deep down in my sockets. And there for so

long, you're almost my first memory. All that came before you
has faded. You're the clear present thing.

NEAL

I'm about as clear as a chemical fog. *(Waits)* But I've waited my
life to hear that much. No soul, live or dead, was ever that kind.

TAW

Not kind, just true—my main hard truth.

Neal suddenly stands but stays in place.

NEAL

Will you drink to that?

TAW

(Waits, surprised; then laughs) Sure. Why not?

Neal turns to the counter to find a clean glass.

TAW

(Holds up Cody's glass) I'll drink after Cody.

*Neal takes Cody's glass, downs the last swallow; then pours Taw
a small drink.*

NEAL

You want it with ice?

TAW

How would I know, friend?

NEAL

I think you're man enough to handle it straight.

*Neal sits again, pours himself a short drink and lifts the glass
toward Taw.*

TAW

Who to? You say.

NEAL

The girl that saved my life years ago.

TAW

Taw Sefton, that girl?

NEAL

The same and only.

TAW

Is anything the same?

NEAL

You. That's been my point for years.

TAW

Can I drink to myself?

NEAL

You'd better.

TAW

All right. *(Turns up the glass and all but drains it, pauses with her head back, then lowers the glass)*

NEAL

Call the doctor?

TAW

(Waits, grins) Call the liquor store. What have I *missed*, all these dry years?

Neal fails to conceal a slight chagrin.

The yard door opens and Porter enters.

Taw shows surprise at his quick return.

PORTER

Baxter's truck blew up at the stoplight; I walked on back.

NEAL

Cody didn't pass you?

PORTER

No.

TAW

He just headed out to the quarry to meet you.

PORTER

Damn. I missed the perfect chance to show him those dismal overpriced apartments and make my offer on this grand house.

NEAL

What can I say?—the gods frown on your enterprise. He'll meet some girl in a pink bikini. They'll dive in the quarry till early dark; then she'll offer a modest *luau* at her new town-house, with sauna to follow.

He'll drive her to South Carolina for the wedding and set her up here in antebellum splendor—hoopskirts and pantalets, slaves fanning flies.

TAW

Porter, sit by me. Drug your nerves.

Porter notices the liquor bottle.

PORTER

Great God!

NEAL

God had nothing to do with this—wed to a *souse*! My head is bowed. Please advise.

Porter finds a glass, then joins them and pours a long drink.

PORTER

Baxter says no way this house'll sell till you fix it up—maybe ten thousand dollars for new beams and roofing. Plus wiring, plumbing, heat-pump and a few more thousand to bring it forward to maybe the *early* twentieth century.

NEAL

If Cody had two grams of sense, he'd contract the job to some good restorer and have himself a treasure. But don't ask me— we're packing tonight and crawling to the Poor House.

Taw takes a long swallow, then sets down her empty glass with grave precision.

TAW

I take dire exception to that, Mr. Avery. Your wife works harder than six queen-bees, and she means to continue. My salary wouldn't keep an anorexic possum, but I sure-God plan to keep *you* in style.

I'll just stride out this afternoon to the trailer park and buy us a beige double-wide mobile home. I'll haul it out to my son's farm by the Brown River, plant a septic tank and put you *in* it— the trailer, not the tank. You won't have to turn a finger till dark. Then *(An expert Mae West imitation)* fire your charcoal and grill my steak.

NEAL

I surrender.

TAW

I refuse your sword just yet—I'm *fighting*.

PORTER

Children, calm your lips. I'm getting a migraine.

The muffled sound of a strong knock at the front door.

TAW

Oh Lord, company—

NEAL

Front-door company. Bound to be the preacher.

PORTER

Want me to head him off?

TAW

Neal, we can't.

NEAL

Tell him I'm prostrate and Taw's in attendance.

TAW

Don't tell a flat lie.

A second louder knock.

NEAL

(To Porter) Say whatever you have to but stop him.

Porter rises, goes through the hall door and shuts it behind him.

Taw rises and gathers the liquor and glasses to hide in the cabinet.

NEAL

(Laughing) Priscilla Mullins, ambushed in sin.

TAW

(Smiling) I know. I deserve it.

Both begin to tidy themselves — hair and clothes.

Taw returns to the table and sits.

As footsteps draw near down the hall, Neal hiccups exaggeratedly.

Taw slaps his hand. They both compose their faces and turn to the door.

The door opens slowly. Porter enters first, then ushers in a tall and meticulously impressive middle-aged man — Fontaine Belfont.

Fontaine takes three steps into the kitchen, stops, looks round carefully, finds Neal and Taw and bows slightly.

PORTER

This is Mr. Belfont. He just arrived.

FONTAINE

Deepest apologies; I know I'm late. I had a bad blowout just up the road.

Neal stands in place.

Taw follows the lead. Seeing that Neal and Porter are baffled, she steps toward Fontaine and offers her hand.

TAW

I'm Taw Avery—Roma's daughter-in-law.

FONTAINE

(Shaking her hand) Fontaine Belfont.

Taw's mouth opens in surprised recognition, but she stands in place and looks back to Neal.

NEAL

(Quietly amazed) From Richmond?

FONTAINE

I was. I'm in Washington now and for the last thirty years—the State Department.

Neal steps round the table and offers his hand.

Fontaine accepts it; then his face contorts in genuine grief.

NEAL

How did you know?

FONTAINE

The obituary.

NEAL

In the *Washington Post?*

FONTAINE

Oh no, your paper. Roma gave me a lifetime subscription years back, so I'd know her news. Somehow I've managed to read it every week—best reading I do.

PORTER

The funniest, I'm sure.

FONTAINE

The headlines are my favorite—"Enraged Woman Bites Off Paramour's Finger, Swallows It."

NEAL

That's in the top ten. My personal favorite is "Mistaken for a Turkey, Egerton Rideout Shot in Face."

All laugh.

Taw waves Fontaine toward the table and a chair.

TAW

Mr. Belfont, you must have missed lunch.

FONTAINE

I admit I did.

Fontaine goes to a chair and sits.

Taw begins to assemble a lunch plate.

Neal and Porter sit.

NEAL

Sounds like you might need a drink. All I've got here is bourbon.

FONTAINE

Ideal—little else touches my lips.

PORTER

No champagne at those treaty signings?

FONTAINE

I'm not in the champagne class, I'm afraid. On the rare occasion we sign one now, I'm more like the man who fills the pens.

Neal goes to the cabinet, resurrects the liquor and finds a clean glass.

NEAL

Water and ice?

FONTAINE

Straight in the glass please—four stiff ounces.

NEAL

I knew I'd like you.

FONTAINE

I doubt you recall but we met one morning, thirty-odd years

back at this same table, I believe I was peddling Bibles at the time.

NEAL

You were. I seem to recall you took my order for the Family Edition, in white leatherette—which I've yet to receive.

FONTAINE

(*Laughs*) I'll look into that.

NEAL

Much obliged—my family's suffered the lack.

Fontaine takes a long swallow of bourbon. Then again he carefully looks round the room.

FONTAINE

It's barely changed.

NEAL

Mother was a staunch opponent of change. I had to rope and tie her to get indoor plumbing, and that was well into modern times.

FONTAINE

I remember the privy; it's where I discovered the works of Willa Cather.

NEAL

Her favorite author. When was your last visit?

FONTAINE

Nineteen forty-six.

NEAL

(*Looks round*) Well, the toaster's new.

Taw brings a loaded plate to the table.

TAW

And the microwave. She said that's exactly what ruined her eyes.

FONTAINE

I know she went blind. How long ago was it?

NEAL

Nearly three years.

TAW

Three years last April. Would you like some tea? It's cold anyhow.

FONTAINE

Thank you, no; I'll stick to firewater. *(Unabashedly bows his head in silence to bless the food, then begins to eat)* Her last letter said she was losing her eyes. I called and said we'd keep in touch on the telephone, but she said "No. This is plain good-bye. We saw each other at our handsome best; let's honor that."

So I honored her word, hard as it was—she knew her own mind well as any Russian premier. I just sent Christmas cards after that.

Taw goes to the sink and begins to work, though closely following the conversation.

NEAL

When the first card arrived, that's when she told me what a friend you'd been.

FONTAINE

(Faces Neal squarely, waits a long moment) I enjoyed Roma Avery thoroughly.

NEAL

She returned the sentiment, sir—I *know.*

FONTAINE

(Waits) Abundant thanks. She never quite said.

NEAL

Thanks were hard for Mother. She lived by acts. If she let you cross her doorsill, she liked you—a very great deal. She didn't have more than two or three virtues, didn't want major virtues, but loyalty was one. I doubt she forgot the dirtiest dog that licked her hand in early childhood.

FONTAINE

(Nods, smiling; another long wait) She gave me this house.

Neal, Taw and Porter are silently stunned. Though they look to one another, none can speak first.

FONTAINE

(Draws an envelope from the inside pocket of his coat) That same last letter. *(Opens the envelope, hunts out the sentence and reads)* "Once you said you'd been happy in this house. From the time my grandfather built it, I'm sure you were the first live human to give it that praise. I want you to have it, the day I die. You can retire to the country and vegetate or burn it, if need be, or give it to somebody else I loved; but don't ever sell it. I can't make other arrangements where I'm going—Hell-fire, I know—but I *can* save my house. I won't have a stranger fouling my beds." *(Extends the pages to Neal)*

NEAL

(His hand hesitates outward, then withdraws) She'd die if I read her mail.

TAW

Neal, she's dead.

NEAL

(With sudden force) So you'd especially like to believe. Roma Avery's *here* and we can't stop her.

Taw hesitates, then chooses to laugh; neither she nor Neal is able to speak.

PORTER

Mr. Belfont, there's a problem here. Mrs. Avery left a legal will, made three months ago. Her grandson Cody inherits this house and most of her holdings.

FONTAINE

(A tactful wait, with blank-faced looks at Neal and Taw) I expected as much.

NEAL

Cody flew home last night from Vietnam — a Purple-Heart Marine.

TAW

He's due back any minute.

FONTAINE

Then we won't mention this. *(Refolds the letter, returns it to his pocket and searches the room with his eyes again)* It is a stout house.

PORTER

I'm hoping to buy it, for my own retirement. I've been in the Navy most of my life; thought I'd come back here and rebuild it. I roomed here for years and was happy too — I doubt I ever told Miss Roma.

NEAL

Not to my knowledge. *I* never did.

Another silent wait. The room dims almost imperceptibly, no rhythmic break. Then Fontaine and Porter speak private truths, unheard by the others.

FONTAINE

I dreamed I could somehow redeem my life, here where I loved this hard old woman. I imagined a place like my childhood, still enough to sleep in and thronged with the ghosts of all I loved. I saw myself amounting to something one last time, as I did for Roma.

PORTER

In this big house long years ago, I prized Neal Avery more than the world. Then I saw the world while he stayed home. No one I met ever gave me more. If I bring what's left of me back now, can Neal — and Taw and maybe Cody — open this circle and let me in?

At the sound of Cody's car in the yard, light rises slowly. All the faces return to the world.

Fontaine returns to his plate and eats.

Neal rises to find new glasses, then pours fresh drinks.

Taw goes to the counter and checks the food.

Cody enters through the yard door, smiling.

CODY

The Mekong Delta is cool as Switzerland next to this. *(Sees Fontaine and stops)*

NEAL

Son, meet an old friend of your grandmother's — Mr. Belfont from Washington.

FONTAINE

(Stands) Fontaine Belfont. You've got Roma's eyes.

Cody waits a long moment and begins to comprehend. He looks first to Neal to confirm his guess. Then he smiles, steps forward and offers his hand.

Fontaine shakes it firmly.

CODY

You just get in?

FONTAINE

(Nods) I had a bad blowout at South Hill, Virginia.

CODY

(Waits) I'm sure she knows you made it this far.

FONTAINE

Many thanks, sir. I'll try to believe you.

CODY

Sit down please. *(Touches the bottle and turns to Taw, who is back at the table)* You planning a saloon? I'll bring you some red-dragon lamps from Nam, some foxy bar-girls in silk hot-pants.

TAW

By all means. *Quick.*

Cody takes a chair from the corner and joins them.

Neal pours a drink and hands it to Cody.

CODY

(Holds the glass out before him) To one grand lady—Roma Avery—the last of the heroes.

All the men nod and drink.

Taw hesitates.

CODY

(Gravely to Taw) I managed to love her.

TAW

(Waits, then nods) I can bow to that. *(Takes a short swallow)*

CODY

(Smiles) Justifies my trip.

Taw nods acceptance and matches his smile.

NEAL

Son, Mother gave Fontaine this house—

FONTAINE

Don't please—

NEAL

Cody's interested in facts.

CODY

(To Fontaine, smiling) Absolutely no problem.

FONTAINE

She said it in a letter years back. I understand there's a more recent will and I fully concur. Roma said more than once how much you meant, how she'd waited for you.

CODY

(Takes a short swallow, then studies Fontaine) Sir, excuse a few questions.

Fontaine nods.

NEAL

Steady, boy.

CODY

Are you somebody Grandmother met in Richmond?

FONTAINE

Somebody? *(Laughs)* I was one young man, at the Jefferson Hotel, late November, in nineteen forty.

CODY

In a black tuxedo?

FONTAINE

(Laughs) I'd come to a dance, but my date got plowed quite early on rum, and I took her home. By the time I came back, all the other girls were also reeling; so I prowled the lobby and joined a bridge game with three old millionaires who lived at the place.

Your grandmother stepped from the dining room at ten o'clock and sat by a lamp, beginning to read. She looked like a statue of Self-Sufficiency high on a temple. I thought "This lady owns herself"—I'd never seen such utter *possession* in a human face. And young as I was, I knew that was something I needed to watch at closer range, so I quit the game I was almost winning and walked over toward her.

She glanced up and said "Young man, you rather resemble *God*." I was taller then with plentiful hair, but I thought she might have been into the sherry. Once I recovered though, I fell down laughing. Roma joined right in and I gave her my heart.

I honestly think she gave me hers, till you came along; then I knew I'd lost to a better rival. Truth to say, by then, it was no great wound. We kept in touch but I told you that. And when I learned she was truly gone, I saw my duty for once and am here.

CODY

(Waits) She wants me to thank you, very deeply, sir.

FONTAINE

(Smiles) Tell her, sir, the pleasure is mine—was and is.

CODY

Your family alive?

Taw registers the strangeness of the question, puts a restraining hand to Cody's arm.

FONTAINE

No kin above ground—no wife, no child.

CODY

Where do you work now?

FONTAINE

Our ever-glorious State Department—a stuffed functionary, a great disappointment. I hope to retire sometime next year.

CODY

(Studies the room for the first time today, then turns to Fontaine) Move in here.

Neal, Taw and Fontaine are stunned, though again in silence.

Porter especially deplores the tack, though he strains to conceal displeasure.

CODY

She'd love the thought. Tomorrow—next year. Move down here and rest, get to know her better.

FONTAINE

(Waits) Cody, life hasn't recently burdened me with gifts. But I've never felt valued more highly than now. You're Roma's child, plainly. I can tell you, she's proud.

NEAL

Laughing, more likely, fit to split. If Mother loved anything more than a quandary, *I* don't know what.

CODY

Captain Avery knows a quandary when he sees one—he's been in a number, and the stakes were high. This one's a cinch. *(Looks round the table)* The house is mine, right? Speak now or never—*(When no one speaks, he turns to Fontaine)*

When Grandmother had her wits about her, she meant you to have this place you'd enjoyed. I give it to you. Come on— we'll go to the courthouse now. *(Suddenly stands)*

NEAL

Son, it's not that simple.

TAW

The hell it's not.

PORTER

Better call Sam Gibbs. *(To Fontaine)* Her lawyer.

CODY

(To Fontaine) You want it? Say the word—

Fontaine smiles but hesitates.

PORTER

If he doesn't, I do. I'll write the check *now*. *(Fumbles in a pocket and finds his checkbook)*

Everyone senses a perilous crossroads. None of the men knows the next sure step.

TAW

(Tightening the cap on the near-empty bottle and holding it out) Spin the damned bottle. *(Laughs)*

PORTER

Steady, girl—no kissing games.

TAW

A game of *chance*—the way Fate guides us.

CODY

(Laughs, takes the bottle and spins it there on the table before them) Hot damn! *(Loving the risk, he turns to Fontaine)* We could always play a little Russian Roulette, but does Spin-the-Damned-Bottle sound fair to you?

FONTAINE

(Bemused but calm) It's your house, Captain.

PORTER

You're the man here, boy. It's yours to give.

CODY

Fate, Porter, Fate. *(Thinks suddenly of his father; has he harmed Neal?)* Father, stop me if I'm wrong—

NEAL

(Waits and looks round) To my great surprise, I can't see how. One big thing's sure—Roma Avery can't lose. Everybody she loved'll be in the game.

TAW

(Clearly but with no rancor) That eliminates me.

NEAL

Goddammit, Taw—Mother proved she loved you, ten thousand dollars worth. You need a valentine?

Taw laughs and accepts her place in the game.

Cody is fully excited by now. He busies himself arranging all chairs, assuring each player space for the game. When the others are set, Cody still stands. He leans in, lays the bottle on its side and prepares to spin.

NEAL

Whoa, son. You too.

CODY

Sir?

NEAL

Remember the will; you're in this too.

FONTAINE

If you're not, I can't play.

PORTER

Absolutely. Me either.

Cody thinks for a moment and seats himself.

CODY

Now who should spin?

When no one volunteers, Neal accepts.

NEAL

Me—nobody living was born here but me.

All note their agreement. By now a real gravity has settled on each, a hushed expectancy but no skittish laughter.

Neal shuts his eyes and faces the ceiling.

NEAL

Mother, one last time—end this *right*.

CODY

Please ma'm.

Eyes still shut, Neal looks down, finds the bottle with his hand and gives a strong spin.

Before the bottle stops, all eyes are shut, all faces turned upward.

When the sound subsides, Cody takes the first look.

CODY

Me.

The others look; then all look to Cody.

FONTAINE

(To Neal) There—Roma heard you.

NEAL

Apparently.

However elated, what follows to the end must not be rushed.

TAW

(Moved) Son, it means —

CODY

(Hushing his mother with a hand, he rises, smiling calmly) It
means I'm free. Mr. Belfont, again I give it to you.

FONTAINE

Again I'm honored, more than you know. Tell me *why* please,
again.

CODY

You gave her the most.

TAW

Son, your father gave her pure heart's *blood.*

CODY

That was his plain duty. *(To Neal calmly)* Sir, am I wrong?

NEAL

(Waits, then smiles) No, love and duty. I quit my claim.

CODY

(To Fontaine) Then one more time, sir—you *held* her, of your
own free will.

FONTAINE

(Standing) Cody, I *did*. *(Waits)* I can swear to that.

CODY

No shadow of doubt.

FONTAINE

(Reaches forward and lays a hand on Cody) You sure she
approves?

CODY

You saw the result.

FONTAINE

(Withdraws his hand) Does any soul, here present, object?

Fontaine looks to each face; each consents.

FONTAINE

I accept. Endless thanks.

Neal rights the bottle, unscrews the cap and begins to portion out the last bourbon.

FONTAINE

Porter, I notice you don't wear a ring.

PORTER

I had a bloodstone that belonged to my father, but it fell overboard in sight of Gibraltar.

FONTAINE

No wedding band.

PORTER

(Holds up a bare hand) One more slave of freedom, single as you.

FONTAINE

(Still to Porter) Could we divide this space in peace—co-owners, on equal terms? I hope to travel most of the year.

PORTER

The old mind boggles—

CODY

Don't think; say yes. I can visit you both, me and sixteen kids, if I come home alive with functional nuts.

TAW

Cody! *(Then laughs)* Don't expect me to cook.

NEAL

I'll cook.

TAW

You can't cook a peeled potato.

NEAL

I can learn.

A general pause of relaxation—grins, swallows of bourbon.

PORTER

Neal, I'll teach you.

TAW

Eternity wouldn't be long enough.

NEAL

(Smiles) Very likely not. One thing I *can* do, here and now — I can make a toast. *(Rises in place and extends his glass)* To this sad house — may it know better days, with all here present and those they love.

ALL

(Severally) Better days. To all here present. And to all we love.

All drink to that and Neal sits.

A sudden cloud obscures the sun. The room darkens slightly and a long chord sounds, tonic and resolved. It is Roma's new voice — no words, new music, confirming Cody's gift and Neal's hope.

Then, enclosed in private light, Taw, Cody and Neal speak their thoughts.

TAW

There's slim hope of this.

CODY

Will I ever see this house again or these welcome faces?

NEAL

I'm the one with hope. Who'd have ever guessed that? Roma Avery's son, the world's oldest boy. There's time for us all. I can see that far.

A trace of normal light returns but, from here to the end, the room is dim. Only faces are clear.

NEAL

(Still seated and quiet) Better days —

CODY

(Both hands up in benediction) Amen, amen.

All extend at least one hand; each hand touches all.

ALL

(Severally and quiet but clear) To be sure. Indeed. Better days. Amen.

Then slowly, with slowly dimming voices, all of them freeze— toasting, smiling—as dark floods the room.

Production Notes

New Music is best seen in sequence, right through on a single afternoon and evening. At its first production, by the Cleveland Play House in 1989, stage time for the three parts was five hours—92, 92, and 126 minutes. With a half-hour intermission between *August Snow* and *Night Dance*, and a 90-minute pause for dinner before *Better Days*, a full performance takes seven hours.

One fluid set will serve throughout—sparely furnished areas for recurrent rooms and one or two neutral spaces for elsewhere. Genevieve's house and Roma's kitchen, for instance, are constant through *August Snow* and *Night Dance*, with small changes in the eight-year gap. Since *Better Days* is set in Roma's kitchen, with moments in two nearby bedrooms, the kitchen may be subtly enlarged.

Place and time are given as North Carolina in the midst of this century. In the upper South of those years, before wide contact with a larger world, an ancient and prodigal strain of the English language was a birthright to every native. For more than three centuries, its power was lavishly spent by people who often lacked other coinage—for care and loathing, to maim or heal. Mostly they spoke in a constant exchange of story and parable—the appalling heroic tales of one talking species adrift on Earth.

The acts and words of *New Music* start at least in that life-or-death need to face and bend reality with speech. But the aim is not for a polished mirror of a land-locked time. All speech and action hope to move further and find, in one family's long discord, a broadly useful harmony—a new old music and the dance it stirs.

Unless all actors are native to the region, an effort to mimic precise accents is likely to fail. Avoid "stage-Southern" dialects, above all the fake-hillbilly nasal twang so often assumed by strangers—*Whīte īce at a nīce prīce.* But note each character's private rhythms and the steady build of longer speeches. Ease the *-ing* endings off participles and adjectives, as most Americans do in conversation. And recall that Southerners often end a sentence with a slight vocal rise, almost a question, in hopes of drawing a listener on.

Try for the implicit whole atmosphere, a close but loose-limbed family of kin and friends who circle in earnest and meet intensely through four decades of a world that changes more rapidly than they. The people differ in origin, station, expressive skills and hopes; but each is formed by the central demand of an old civilization—its codes of courtesy, loyalty, honor and mercy. Recall that most dialects of the South are founded upon the first principle of thoughtful discourse everywhere—*Be as clear and entertaining as truth and brevity allow (and if the truth is boring, don't hesitate to stretch it).*

The South was, and is, a society like others in which hot violence is elaborately hid but coiled to strike—northern Ireland, Sicily, the Middle East, Men and women encounter each other with provisional trust that may instantly flare into danger or death at a hint of trespass or betrayal. But in daily encounters, a harshly raised voice is seldom heard, much less the exasperated irony and insult of many American urban dialects. Here passion, pain or threat is mostly conveyed by clear-eyed eloquence, wit, rhythm, light emphasis and restrained gesture. That struggle to talk, not kill, can lend an armed power to the simplest transaction.

Clothing is of good, though not luxurious, quality. Fashions will be a year or so late. With the exception of Dob Watkins, all are conscious of clothes as another means of diverting and taming the world. Again avoid stereotypes—no white linen suits and string ties for the men, no picture hats or chiffons for the women.

Each play occurs in late summer. In the absence of air conditioning, a towering heat and humidity weigh on speech and action.

Radio was a frequent presence in rooms. So popular band and vocal music of the time—jazz, swing and boogie, romantic ballads, black gospel, blues and rock—may be used to strong effect, provided no meanings are drowned. A striking contrast can be made in *Better Days* between the gentle folk rock of the sixties and the Vietnam-stained rock that ensued.

About The Author

Reynolds Price was born in Macon, North Carolina in 1933. He was reared and educated in his native state, taking his A.B. from Duke University. In 1955 he traveled to Merton College, Oxford where he studied for three years as a Rhodes Scholar. He then returned to Duke and began the teaching which he continues as James B. Duke Professor of English.

In 1962 his first novel *A Long and Happy Life* appeared. It received the William Faulkner Award and has never been out of print. In ensuing years he has published seven more novels, most recently *The Tongues of Angels*. In 1986 his *Kate Vaiden* received the National Book Critics Circle Award. He has also published volumes of short stories, poems, plays, essays, translations from the Bible and a memoir, *Clear Pictures*.

He wrote his first play *The Wise Men* at age thirteen. In 1978 *Early Dark* was produced at the WPA Theatre in New York. His television play *Private Contentment* was commissioned by American Playhouse for it first season in 1982, and in 1989 his trilogy *New Music* premiered at the Cleveland Play House. *Full Moon*, commissioned and performed by Duke

Drama, had its first professional production at New Stage, Jackson, Mississippi in 1990.

He is a member of the National Academy and Institute of Arts and Letters. His books have appeared in sixteen languages.